PASSPORT TO ME

PASSPORT TO ME

EVELYN C. WALSH

CreateSpace
New York

FIRST EDITION

All rights reserved, including the right of reproduction in whole or in part in any form.

Copyright © 2015 by Evelyn C. Walsh

ISBN: 0991358325
ISBN 13: 9780991358328
Library of Congress Control Number: 2015902312
Evelyn C. Walsh Sole Proprietor, New York, NY

For My Readers

TABLE OF CONTENTS

Acknowledgements	xv
The Affair	1
Aging	2
Alice	4
Always I	6
Always II	7
Always III	9
And Greater Things Shalt Thou Do	11
Angel and Camden	12
Anguish	13
Anna Washburn	14
April	15
Aries Rising	16
Assisi	17
Athens. The Olympics.	18
The Attic	19
Authenticity	21
Being Old	22
Beloved Heroes	23
Beloved Moments	26
Ben	27
The Best Language	29
Bethel, Vermont	30

Betsy	31
Bird Dance	33
Birthday Poem	34
Blink	35
Boundaries	36
Brenda	37
Bridget's Hearth	38
Burned Bridges	39
Bystanders of the 60s	41
The Card Girl	42
Carlow	44
Cat Partner	46
Cat Tale	47
A Catskill Thanksgiving	49
Certainty	52
The Channeled Life	53
Charlie	54
The Chattering Mind	55
Choices	56
Christmas Cards	57
Christmas in Ireland	59
Christmas Snow	61
A Christmas Story	62
Clarity	63
Clouds	64
Clover Bunny	65
The Comet Kohoutek	66
The Community Gardens	67
Continuity	68
The Cosmic Internet	69
Cosmic Love	70
Cosmic Security	72
The Courage of Christopher Reeve, Actor Activist	73

Daddy	74
Daisy	75
Daphne	77
Dear Old Bill	78
Debts	79
Dedicated to Anne McManus	80
Dinner at Daphne's	81
Divinity	82
Divorce	83
Dogs or Cats?	84
The Doorman	85
Dublin City	86
Dying	89
Earth Planet	90
The Easter Bunny	91
Easter Visit	92
Eighty-One and Counting	93
Eire	94
Empathy	96
The Extra Mile	97
Fall	98
The Fan Club	99
The Farm	100
Fear	101
Feelings	102
For Dorothy	103
For Georgia	104
For Twins	105
Forgiveness	106
Forsythia	107
A Glimpse of Heaven	108
Going Going Gone	109
Good Friday	110

Grandmas	112
Grief	113
Growing Old	114
Guilt	115
Halley	116
A Handshake or a Kiss	118
Heather Hills in Ireland	119
Heaven	121
Heaven Here	122
Heaven on Earth	123
Heidi … A Mountan Goat	124
Henry	126
Here's to Comedians	128
Hizzoner the Hero	129
Hostage	131
How Sweet It Is	132
I Don't Have to Know	133
I Have Chosen You	134
The Internet Romance	135
Interplanetary Connections	136
Ireland	137
Irish Spring	138
It's Gone	139
Joanne	140
Johnny	142
Josephine	143
A Journey	144
Junie	146
Knowing Hell	148
Labor Day 1980	149
Last Will and Testament	150
Legacies	151
A Letter to Heaven	152

Lift-Off	153
Limited Partnership	155
A Line at a Time	156
Linger	157
Loves	158
Luck	159
Made in Vermont	160
Maggie	162
Management by Objective	163
Manhattan Snowfall	165
Marion	167
The Marriage	169
Martyrdom	172
Master of Time	173
May Days … A Trip	174
Me	176
Memories of Aunt Ruth	177
Memories of Chile	179
Mona Lisa	181
Mother's Day	182
Mt. Lympus	183
Musical Memories	184
My Double	185
My Room	186
My Sister's Garden	187
Now	188
October	189
October 12, 2004	190
October Visit	192
Ode to a Bygone Summer	193
Ode to the Farm	194
OD'ed on Sorrow	195
The Office	196

Old Age	197
The Olympics	198
On Being a Twin	199
On Retirement	200
Oo Lee	202
An Open Book	205
An Ordinary Day	206
Our Vermont Farm	208
The Patience Medal	210
Patterns by Stella	211
Pavarotti	212
Peace in Me	213
Persistence	214
Pessimism	215
Philanthropy	216
Pisces	217
Plateful of Stress	218
Play It Again, Please	220
Poetry and Life	221
Pokey Paterno	223
The Power of Choice	225
Pregnant	226
The Price of a Poem	227
Project Plan	228
Refuge	229
Remember	230
Remembrance	231
Resurrection Day	233
The Reunion	234
Riverside Park	236
Robyn	237
Rockefeller Center Christmas Tree	238
Rose	240

Ruins	241
The Sacred Heart	243
Saturday Mornings	244
The Sea of the Mind	245
Sea Shells	246
The Shadow	247
Shadows	248
A Silent Experience	249
The Simple Life	250
Some Things We'll Never Know	251
Somebody to Buy Candy for	252
Somerset	253
Soul Sight	254
The Spiral of Time	255
Spiritual Legacy	256
Spring	257
Still the Stars Shine	258
Stillness	264
Stonehenge	266
Sully	267
Take It to My Soul	269
Take Me to Ireland	271
Telepathy	272
Tell Me Why You Like It Here	273
Thanksgiving Day 1983	274
34	276
Time	277
Time is the Pen	278
Timeless Truths	279
To One Another on Our Golden Wedding Anniversary	280
Together Again	282
Traditions of Christmas	283
Trouble	284

Truth	285
Twin	286
Understand Me	287
United Nations Garden	288
University of Adversity	289
Vermont	290
The Vermonter	291
Veterans Day	293
The Vibration of the Day	294
Vivid Experience	295
War Backpack	296
Watching the Clock	298
Waters of Sorrow	300
We Need More Irish Days	301
What If Now Is Heaven?	302
What Is	303
What's It Like at 75?	304
White Rabbit	305
Wild Flowers	306
Workmates	307
Work Partners	308
The Writing Process	309
Zene Dekalim	310
The Zoo Girl	311
About the Author	313

ACKNOWLEDGEMENTS

This book could not have come to life without the technical assistance and friendship of Karen Hadam, Nancy Morrison and Robert Fischer. My warmest thanks and love.

THE AFFAIR

They had an affair.
One that lasted
A lifetime.
A carryover from lives
Lived before
In distant lands
Soon to be seen again.

It was not an affair of the body
But of the mind and the spirit.
Their talents were different.
Complemented one another
Synchronized.
Work partners
Play partners, too.

They were not understood by many
Indeed misunderstood.
But not by one another.

A love shared
That enriched their lives
And inspired them to be more.
Now and always.
Best friends.

AGING

Aging on her mind
Three Score and Ten
On the horizon.
She liked
The perspective
Aging brings
The panorama
Of her life
Spread across the years
Like a book
Upon which to reflect.
Still time for
More chapters
She hoped.
But if not
She stood by
Her choices.
She'd been true
To her heart –
Her decision-maker.
Sometimes it chose duty
When she'd rather it had not
But she'd always known
Her heart knew best
And time would
Prove its worth.

It did not save from sorrows
Of these she'd
Had some deep
But choices
Trusted to the heart
Were ones
She still could keep.
Regrets there were
Omissions some
She'd change them
If she could
But none so large
At least to her
As to be misunderstood.
Better to like yourself
She thought
Forgive the wrongs you've done
The record of your life is writ
And cannot be undone.

ALICE
(For Alice Grillo)

I was always looking for an Alice of my own.
The name conjured
Blue gowns. Fancy balls.
Gentleness.
A lady.
An aura of light
Her face shown
I'll always remember that about her.
Her luminosity. Her positivity. Creativity.
Knitting in her hospital room.
A cozy one.
Thinking of the future.
Planning for the future.
Looking smashing.
In a pink gown actually.
Never mind. Just as nice as blue.
She was gallant in adversity. Serene.
Still furious at the insensitive
Often slow help for the really ill.
She rose above it all. Fixed it for herself
With the aid of family and friends.
Ever the good witness
For all those who had disappointed me
She stood. And served.
On the bedside table
Two red roses with baby's breath
A crystal vase
Slender red ribbon entwined.

We visited
As old friends do
And kissed we knew good-bye
With a tear and a smile
Until just but awhile
And a firm gait
On parting
'Til then.
All my days will include her
So proud she will be
When next we're together
In eternity.

ALWAYS I

They said goodbye
In the office
Where they had met.
They would not meet again
It was not to be
In this life.
But it was for always he'd pledged
And she believed him.
It was a generation more
Before they met again
In another place
Both having been born again
Into new worlds.
Time to fall in love again.

ALWAYS II

Never alone
A wall of love
Around me
Always he'd said
Together forever
No matter
How far apart
Dimensions separated them
New lives for each
But she knew
His love was near
She felt it
When she talked
With him
In the language of love
That knows no bounds
No spoken words
To make it real.
Always.
She believed him
And claimed
The promise.
Nothing could
Separate her
From his love.
From incarnation
To incarnation

It was here
Because love travels
Through time and space
Always mine.

ALWAYS III

I wonder if he really had thought about Always.
I'll always love you, he said.
Dead now 26 years.
Does he love me now?

"Always" he signed letters and cards.
Even before he was terminally ill.
How could he know this?
I pondered.

I was reluctant to commit
Myself to Always.
Together forever?
What if I changed my mind?
After all, I'd fallen out of love before.

But he was an Aquarian
And probably meant it
In a more universal way.

Surely we would love one another
Always
Together or apart
In ways we both understood.

I believe we will meet again
To continue what
We'd begun
In time.

Because I believed him.

AND GREATER THINGS SHALT THOU DO

He came to save the lost
But first the lost became
To share in the experience
Of becoming human
Whose life on earth
Showed not what God
But man could do right then
To be as humanly divine
As all men can become
To take responsibility for
Dying for one's self
So we can join Him now
With those before and after
Who have shown us how
To make a heaven of the earth
That needs no Gods to do
But only those who understand
That we can do it, too.

ANGEL AND CAMDEN
(For Andree and Baerbel)

It was so impossible a tale
That it had to be true.
Or was our credulity being tested?
Some might say our imagination
Being stirred
By a wild story
From the Old West.

We'd just gotten our Merlot at the midtown
Outdoor café
When the woman at the next table
Asked if she might query three wise women
For advice about impending motherhood.
At 47.
An experience she'd chosen by adoption.
Two babies, ten weeks and sixteen months.

We listened enthralled
As outrageous often is.
Seductive. Entertaining. Worrisome.
We gave sound advice.
Why, it might even be true.
Congratulations.

In *vino veritas*? Or just plain tight.
We three believed not in accidents.
Only incidences
So, we pondered these things
As women of old.

ANGUISH

Anguish enveloped her
Squeezed hard and held
Sorrow and sadness
Rained down.
So poignant the moment
Understanding
Gave comfort
To anguish
Made her see
What it was
She missed.
What it was
From long ago
That she needed now
Bring it back to me
She asked
That feeling that
She once and always knew
She could come home
Again.

ANNA WASHBURN

She was a Vermonter
Of more than 90 years
Few had her memories
Of a time still clear
But lost to us
Who'd come to hear
Of days gone by
Now history
That we knew not
But missed
That her stories
Brought near.
Gone from our midst
But a legacy remains
Of a Vermont,
And Anna
We hold dear.

APRIL

A banner year for lilacs
Blooming in the spring
Announcing its arrival
A new year to begin.
A season rife for planting
Asks us to reply
In perennials multi-colored
Our joy to multiply.
Daffodils first. Then Tulips.
Primroses. Pansies, too.
Azaleas. Iris. Peonies.
Fuchsias and Geraniums.
Petunias of varied hue
Make spring a time of growing
Nature gives to you.

ARIES RISING

Dawn had not yet come to Lympus, Vermont
The farm sat high on the hill
It was early fall
The trees turning faster now
After the first frost.
I'd made the fire
In the kitchen wood stove
And the coffee
Sat down at the big table
By the windows
To watch morning come.
Morning whispers to me
In the dark of night
That soon she will be here
And I must rise to greet her
As for a friend most dear.
Few greater joys
Are there to me
Than darkness turn to day
To see first light
An endless thrill
I cannot turn away.
Whether sun or clouds
Rain or mist
The frost or snow to see
The sky remains a wonder
A daily mystery
To miss the start of a new day
Is a real loss to me.
May it ever be.
May it ever be.

ASSISI

Give me a mantle of hearts, she asked.
I have a mantle of stones.

Let us go to Assisi
St. Francis to see
We will walk together
There by the Priory.
Along a border of flowers
A chat among the trees
Of thought carried from you to me
On issues,
Ideas, and the like.
The pleasure of the moment
A walk at dawn's first light.

ATHENS. THE OLYMPICS.

The best of the best.
I am drawn to it
Each time.
Special this year
In Greece.

From the eye of decades
One views youth
Glorious bodies
Inspiring dedication
Really hard work
In pursuit of gold.

Sport as art,
The swimmer gliding
Home underwater
Romania on balance beam
Unequaled in freedom
And grace.

THE ATTIC

We could only reach the attic
By a ladder
Pushing aside the small board
Which was its entrance
And scrambling in.
We were small and scared
But not too scared to do it.

It was a wondrous place
Full of special things
We seldom saw.
Old chairs
Dusty with the years
Toys no longer used
Except up there
Where we'd ride
The kiddie car
The length of the attic.
Trunks and boxes of old clothes
Old clocks
And bric-a-brac.
Forbidden territory
We loved to explore
When Mother was away.
In the same way
We learned to smoke
Lighting our stolen cigarettes
On the kitchen stove
Sitting on the front steps

So as not to smell up the house.
We got caught anyway
Because we smelled up ourselves.
But it was another adventure
From a happy childhood
Still remembered
And treasured.

AUTHENTICITY

She felt a poem stirring
Deep within
When it finally arrived
She was always surprised
Much like giving birth.
The pain soon forgotten
By the wonder of the child.

In the quiet of the
Early morning
Inspiration came
'Twas then she
Reached for pen
Only when her spirit spoke
Did the poem begin.

Others have a different style
Write from eight 'til ten
I cannot tell you
Which is yours.
Try until you find
Authenticity the key
Will be the cosmic sign.

BEING OLD

A lot of it
A surprise.
A state unknown
To her
But travelled by many.
She saw them
Every day
On the street
On the bus
In the restaurant
I wonder how old
They are
She asked herself?
Perhaps younger than I.
Am I old she questioned?
Probably.
It had arrived.
Rather unnoticed
Until seats on the subway
And bus became routine.
I must be old.
Really.
Funny
The way
News arrives.

BELOVED HEROES

Police
Firefighters
Emergency Medical Services Personnel
Died for me today
In triumph
Over death
And cruelty
For lack of love
For one another.

We feel now a solidarity
With those who love.

Those who are gone
Are safe now
It is those left behind
Who are not.
Wounded. Hurt. In despair.
We share their pain
Stand in line
To give blood
To volunteer
For anything
We can do to help.
We wait.

When invulnerability died
The investigations proceed
And we process
The data
Into our bodies
As we rise from the dead
To a new life
We must create
To honor the lives lost.

It's back to work tomorrow
Still hopeful.
Keeping vigil.
Lighting candles.
Singing songs.
As heroes toil
Night after day
Against the elements
Uncertainty
Our new companion.

The first Sunday
After becomes
A day
The national family
Mourns
And remembers.
Services
Mark the day.

Sad is here again
The emptiness,
Anguish
Pain
Each sad different
But the same.
Day follows day
Of aching grief.
Sorrow we became.

BELOVED MOMENTS

There must be a way
To relive beloved moments
I didn't notice enough then
She mused.
And she set about it
Having learned
Painfully
That she herself was the creator.
She entered the memory
Merged with it
'Til they were one again.
Alive on the screen
Preserved forever
On her soul.
She could go there.
It was a place
Her soul.
The secret door
To it all.

BEN

We hardly knew him
In our lives a few days
In our Rachel's three weeks
But he is to be a part of our lives always.
Died in Barcelona
Rachel's classmate junior year abroad
They became close
Did everything together
Instant friendship
Interrupted by slight headaches
That became worse
Until one morning
He took a cab to the hospital.
Brain tumor, the doctors said
No family there
He texted Rachel
Come, he said.
She came. Talked with him.
Held his hand. Caressed his arm.
His family came.
Rachel briefed them
Who thanked her profusely.
For being there for Ben.
As she continued to be.
At first there was some hope.
An encapsulated tumor removed
But two others remained.
Now water swelled
And could not be quelled.

Twenty years old
Gentle Ben
Who left us much too soon
An aching void
Of no understanding.
Help us to accept thy will
Oh universe.
And keep Ben close
As he goes on before.
Beloved son
Beloved friend.

THE BEST LANGUAGE

It is silence.
Wordless.
Understood.
Funny how much information
Can be exchanged without
A word being spoken.

BETHEL, VERMONT

It was a summer
Rich in clover
And Queen Anne's Lace.
From behind the lilacs
And the stone wall
Beside the wild roses
My eyes took in it all
Feasting on the meadows
The old apple trees
The dirt and grassy driveway
All are dear to me.
The mountain peak
In distance
Blue against the sky
Filled with puffy pillows
Playfully passing by
The hum of bees on clover
An airplane on high
Country sounds of August
Butterflies nearby.
Maples turning rosy
Blackberries finishing up
The sun shone hot
And warmed my soul.
As nature filled my cup.

BETSY

She always had her lipstick on
Jewelry on her ears
A pretty nightgown
There to see
Ready as she welcomed me.

I brought *The Times* and soup
A different one every day.
She got *The Observer*
The New Yorker and *Vanity Fair* by mail.

We chatted about current events.
But not dying.
Betsy never acknowledged
That death was near.
She lived as normally
As treatments permitted.
Her only complaint
Lack of sleep
But that was lifelong.
She finally accepted a sleeping pill.
She wished she had more energy.

She pushed herself
Through growing weakness
Up the 67 steps to her apartment
Until November 26.

She died December 13.
Bedridden only three days.
The doctor downstairs and I
Made her comfortable.
She took sips of water but no food.

She accepted death now.
Invited it to come
Quickly and quietly.
I stayed by her side
Until she left
As she wished
In her own home
An unspoken agreement we had.

BIRD DANCE

They gathered
At her feet
On the snow
They flew to the near
Dense tree
Back and forth
Up and down
Together
They did a
Dance for me.

BIRTHDAY POEM

I was home to visit
And no one there could guess
How much it was I'd learned away
About happiness.

It was in memories all around me
And I'd come again to fill
My cup of life with water pure
From streams fast running still.

BLINK

Certainty.
Absolute.
Instantly.
No thought needed
All thought
Already done.
Focused now
From knowledge
Experience
Wisdom
Bubbling up
From her subconscious
Certainty.

BOUNDARIES

It was a year of
Setting boundaries
Needed for a long time
But not recognized.
What she thought was a virtue
Turned out to be not
When she saw it,
Owned it,
It could be fixed.
She couldn't do it alone
This she knew
But help came along
And boundaries were new.
Bringing health and freedom
From martyrdom.

BRENDA

There was a sense of serenity.
It was over.
Death had come
To set her free
From months of agony.

She was so good.
So young.
We could not understand
Why death would come so early
To take her by the hand.

But looking at her well-lived life
In many ways complete
We had to accept that
Death was not defeat.

Love had called her home.
For needs that only heaven knew,
May such be said
Of me and you.

BRIDGET'S HEARTH

It was a bit of a surprise
A bit of a romantic surprise
I should say
To see you there
By the fire
Warmin' your hands.
'Tis a fair fire
'Tis, you agreed
And the blue in the flame
Answered true
Moments that passed
As in childhood days
Again were remembered with you.

BURNED BRIDGES

They were discarded.
Obsolete.
Too old, he said to be his friend.
No initiative
Too passive
Non-supportive of his work
He needed new friends
Young ones
Not like us.

It was a mask he wore
We believed in him.
He was that good.
We were overwhelmed
With hurt and confusion
We did not understand
This un-loving friendship.

There are loving ways
To disconnect
Take a sabbatical
From one's life
To make a new one.

Is there a need to ditch the old
Who have been there for you?
Try to remember
The fun we had together
Tainted now by your depression.

True, we are old.
Not just in years
But experience and wisdom
Harvest time.
Old can be fun.

We don't need drama.
Been there. Done that. Spare us.
Respect us.
If new life you seek
You will not find it without the memory of us.

BYSTANDERS OF THE 60S

They still were proud
These bystanders of the 60s
Who only watched
Too frightened to participate
Too inhibited
Or with no belief in themselves
Really.

Many of the best
And the brightest
Plunged in
The status quo not good enough
A risk
But one worth taking
Believing that the universe
Always in charge
And their own best selves
Should be put on the line
For a better future
For all.
They made a difference.

THE CARD GIRL

Herself a greeting card
Daisy in her hand
Brown hair in the wind
Flashing eyes
And laughing mouth
With voice as a clear bell
Walking lightly o'er the green
Wishing all is well.

She comes herself
To visit you
In her greeting card
Get well – Hello
Bon Voyage – Welcome Back
Happy Birthday – Missing You
Happy New Year
Be My Valentine
Happy St. Pat's – Easter Wishes
While You Are in the Hospital
It's Halloween
Thanksgiving – From the Folks at Home
All Saints' Day
Merry Christmas
On Your Engagement – Happy Wedding Day
Gone Fishing
On Your New Apartment

And the card blank for all occasions
Color her green, emerald green
As the grass in the Magic Isle
Claudia Green
The Card Girl.

CARLOW

It was many years later
When the scene came to her again.
Carlow.
Early morning. Late winter.
Frost on the fields.
En route to Dublin.
A rest stop at an old pub.
She had a candy bar from a machine
We met at the Gresham.
The history of the hotel
Surrounded us,
As we drank Irish whiskey
In the lobby
And lied to one another.
I was an observer.
And believer still
Diplomacy observed
While betrayal played out
Unknown to her
Paid for by her.
She doubted this was
A true memory.
But that was the
Essence of it.
Betrayal.
By a friend.

It took years to heal
Unimportant now
She was who she was
And that was the deal.

CAT PARTNER
(For Frisky Steinlauf)

May you travel well
My friend
Mid arbors of violet hue
Wisteria winding o'er wooden limbs
Making curtains surrounding you.
Warm rays of sunlight
Filtering through
The lacey flower bower
As you lazily watch
Through half-closed eyes
A humming bird
Caught on the wing.
This must be heaven
Is this message she'll bring
In the song she will sing
We will often think of you there
May you often think of us
Here.

CAT TALE
(Lambda)

On my mind
The cat who
Lived with me
Thirteen years.
A long life
For his breed
Burmese. Beige. Brown and White.
Round blue eyes.
Considering
A poor start
With a sister
Who died at three months
Lady Guinevere.
A weak sphincter muscle
Plagued Lambda and me all his life.
And kept him out of my bedroom.
It was a game Lambda played
Trying to get into my bedroom
When I forgot to close the door
Which was often.
I spent a lot of time
Remembering to do it.
Lambda was gentle
But his howling
Got to me
And haunts me still.
When there were three cats
Hamlet, Sudi and Lambda,

All was serene.
After their deaths
Lambda's grief
Became howling.
I felt his pain.
Lambda's gone now
And I miss him.
But not his howling.
It comes to me now and again
Very faintly.
And I know he's
Still nearby.
He made it
Onto the bed.

A CATSKILL THANKSGIVING

A tradition of many years now
Thanksgiving in the Catskills
At Wolf Lake.
Home there was called
"Peace of the Lake"
And it was.
Nestled down a stiff drive
Through rhododendron and pine
To the house
Overlooking the lake
Easily seen through
Bare November trees
Sparkling in the sun
Or hidden by fog.
We are cozy within.

There always is an early Christmas tree
Beautifully trimmed
With presents beneath
For the children.
Macy's parade on TV
Accompanied kitchen preparations.
The gathering number about 20
Seated at the festive table.
The smaller children at the connecting card table.
They've grown up now
But still sit there.

First are hors d'oeuvres
Cheeseballs and crackers.
Nuts and pepperoni.
A glass of wine.

We look for our place cards made by the
Children years ago.
Our traditional menu
Not allowed to vary.
Turkey. Mashed potatoes and gravy.
Candied sweet potatoes. Mashed yellow turnips.
Creamed onions. Corn. String beans.
Lima/tomato beans.
Jellied and berry cranberries.
Roasted peppers, olives, pickles.
Burnt rolls.
Cider, milk and wine.

A prayer of Thanksgiving by the host.

The feast.

Afterward a nap for some.
Or a walk around the Lake.
Quadding now for the bold.
A 1,000 piece puzzle.
Or entertainment by the children.

Telephone calls to absent family.
The men do the dishes.
The women put away
The leftovers for take home.

Supper is desserts.
Pies: pumpkin, lemon, apple, pecan.
Whipped cream.
Chocolate chip squares.
Cranberry nut bread.
A cornucopia of chocolates.

In the evening
Those who stay over
Read or watch a movie
The dog at their feet,
A family day
Remembered lovingly
By those who share it
Each Thanksgiving.

CERTAINTY

Her certainty was
Contagious.
She must look anew
At her own.
She had the capacity
To unsettle views
Held a lifetime.
Expose to the light
The certitudes
To watch them felt
To watch them melt
In the sun of love.

THE CHANNELED LIFE

She sought the
Channeled life
Life from above
Moment by moment
Aware of heaven's breath
Spirit within
Reaching upward
Manifesting down
Into my reality.

∼

She went on automaton
Letting others in
To take her life
And live it
Above the worldly din.
Assured it would be perfect
Because every one chipped in
She leaned upon their wisdom
As one with them became.

CHARLIE

A spirit sent from up above
To dwell with you a time
In the body of a child
But a giant of a mind.
He chose two special parents
To bring him to this plane
Because they had the spirit
Where he could feel at home.
Now he has gone on before
To make a place for you
To join him in the sky …
But leaves with you his spirit
The life that cannot die.

THE CHATTERING MIND

She met
This person who
Called herself
The Chattering Mind.
She recognized herself
In the description.
She, too, had a
Chattering mind.
Difficult to silence
Each one of a kind
Detach yourself
Surrender
Let go the
Chattering mind
Send it away
Put it aside
You need not
Let it hold sway.
The choice is mine
To keep or stay
To keep
Or stay
In line.

CHOICES

She wanted to let go
Tried to. Prayed to.
But the tie was too strong.
Too deep.
It reached the marrow of her bones.
It was not her mind
Nor even her heart
But her soul
That was enveloped.
She gave up. Surrendered.
She would have to
Accept the ambiguity.
What frightened her
Was the choice
Her soul would someday make for her.
In spite of her conscious self
Because know she did
That the soul knew all
And that the journey designed with it long ago
Was her yellow brick road.

CHRISTMAS CARDS

She sat on her bed
Where she often read
And wrote.
It was Christmastime
And she was surrounded
By the cards
She wanted to send.
Seals and stamps
The address list
The tradition of years.
She was worried
That she hadn't
Started yet
Here the 15th of December
Today was the day
She insisted.
Once started
She gave herself to it
Wholeheartedly.
Immersed in memories
Of times long past
And current.
There was no more prospect of
Skipping Christmas cards
Than flying.
It was unthinkable.
As long as she was able
There were many who did just that
And sometimes she envied them.

At the same time
She felt sorry
That they would not know
The intensity
The depth
The connectedness
Of the ritual
Over the years
Among family
And friends.
Christmas cards.

CHRISTMAS IN IRELAND

It was Christmas again
In Ireland to spend
She mused
As she gazed at the flame
In the old fireplace
That had seen more than
Three score and ten
Empty for years
Until now we are here
To celebrate Christmas again
In the cottage of Bridget
Within whose stone walls
Memories of Christmases
Decades before
Of some who are here
And some who are not
But still are remembered
When much else forgot.
All the years are as one
As we all meet once more
In a phone call to heaven
Wherever we are.
Love is the connection
For a heart to heart chat
In a phone call from earth
For Christmas at that.
We exchanged Season's Greetings
In abundance of mirth
At the ease of the call

The economy rate
Heart-to-heart
Sweet connection
No trouble at all
Anytime
Free to all
Instant as thought
Sent by the mind
Faster than light
Faster than sound
Happy Christmas. Happy Christmas.
Below as above
Chime the bells
Chime the bells
Area code L-O-V-E
Area code L-O-V-E
Once again
Peace to Men
Peace to Men.

CHRISTMAS SNOW

It started in the night.
Snowflakes for Christmas.
Awake at four
She went to the kitchen window
To see them tumbling down
For the first time in ages
On Christmas Day.

What a wonderful treat,
She thought.
It snowed all day
Working up to a storm
Hindering travel
Canceling visits.

We were snowed in.
Worrying about those
Out in it.

Nature forced a time out.
A celestial slowdown.
Nature still king.

A CHRISTMAS STORY

I met the Holy Ghost again
The morn of Christmas Eve
The Holy Ghost of Simeon
Who whispered in his ear
That he would see the Christ child
Before his time to leave.
This Holy Ghost who whispers
Comes to me today
With an ancient story
Whence time does not hold sway.
The story of the Holy Ghost
Who lives within each one
Seen by those who've pierced the veil
'Twixt earth and heavenly homes.

CLARITY

Flashed on her mind
From time to time
She tended to Neptunalize
Dream of it
As she wished it to be
The reality
Transformed
Into the dream.
It was a long time
Before she saw it
And she was pleased
She had not seen it
Sooner.

CLOUDS

She'd always loved
White puffy clouds
Pillows in the sky.
No painter could ever
Capture their
Multi-faceted arrangements
Edifices no architect
Could design
Sailing full mast
Across the
Ice blue sky.
Lacy clouds
Spidery ones
Fans and ferns
Some appearing
To pause
And rest
Atop the trees.

CLOVER BUNNY

I could scarcely believe it.
A bunny not five feet away.
Munching clover,
Intent on his food
He did not move
As I stood stock still
And felt the thrill
Of a presence
I can re-create at will.

THE COMET KOHOUTEK

With all the power of
The Bride of the Lamb
I called you.

It was not enough.

More power.
More power.
Alternating power.
Hexagon power.

I reached for the connection
Across the abyss of time
And found you.

Rushing through space
To meet me.

With molecules of eternal life.

THE COMMUNITY GARDENS

Lonely for a poem
Was how she felt.
And one came running.

Dusty rose daisies
Spring swept.
Wind swept.
In the community garden
Riverside Park
On the old Westside highway
Parallel the Hudson
Where often they walked
And watched the seasons change.

In a city of millions
Sometimes alone.
While they loved the solitude
They wondered
At the priorities of others
Who could – but did not
Come to nature's joys.

Birdsong.
The perfume and beauty of flowers.
The sun on our faces.
Clouds
Hawks circling in the sky
Enveloped in nature's bounty
Herein peace lies.

CONTINUITY

Life continues
Going forward
It looks backward
At memories in time
That fill the heart
Cannot be left behind.
History.
How precious it was
How precious it is
To remember
And relive it again
Like a record
To play
On the screen of my mind
An imprint
Forever
Recalled when inclined.

THE COSMIC INTERNET

I dialed you up, darling
Easy it was.
Just said your name
Three times
In my mind
From my heart
And we were connected
Sweet mystery
Sheer ecstasy
Brings you back
To me.

COSMIC LOVE

Her heart reached
Across time
Searching for him
In infinity
Like E.T.
A phone call home.

When they were connected
She asked him to come to her in a dream.

He wanted to come live
But she was still too afraid.

She knew it could be done
Because others she believed in
Had had the experience
But she was not ready.

Dreams she thought
Would help her
And she was just now
Learning about dreams
From Carl Jung
Whose spirit was
Close to her own.

She told her lover all this
And felt his love envelop her.

On earth

As it continues

In the heavens.

COSMIC SECURITY

I walked along the
Old Westside Highway
In late summer.
The sky blue
No clouds
On this early September morn
2005.
This heaven is not guaranteed
I thought.
Remember Katrina
Soak it in.
It may not come again
For me.

I have this moment
With what will I fill it?
Only my favorite things
I must make my own heaven
I am a co-creator
With the universe
With my now
I'll make it swell.
Understanding the laws of the universe.
Cosmic security.

THE COURAGE OF CHRISTOPHER REEVE, ACTOR ACTIVIST
(A Tribute)

Now he was Courage
Christopher Reeve.
Worthy of Superman.
Who left for higher planes
Today
His work here done
Victory won.
A life well lived
To be remembered long
In words and song
For the courage
To discover life anew.
An icon of courage.

DADDY

Why can't I write about him,
I wondered.
I miss him more, not less
As years go by.
He was a wonderful father
Supportive. Protective.
His corny jokes
Remembered with affection.
His integrity well known
In our small town
Where he had been
Building Inspector
For thirty-seven years
Inspires me still.
His unconditional love
Was a shield for me
Against adversity.
I can hear him as he lay dying
In the parlor.
"You can always come home, Bud."
He was the only one
Who called me Bud.
It matters not that heaven is his home now.
I know that I can still go home.

DAISY
(The One With The Waggily Tail)

We got her at the Pound
Hanna's dog.
I wanted her to get some exercise
And to have company.
We had to fill out forms
And wait a long time
We watched the cats
In their cages against the wall
While we waited.
Hanna had had a cat
Frisky. Black and white.
I thought perhaps
She'd rather have a cat
But she said no.
In fact
She was ready to forget about a pet
She was getting nervous waiting
But I insisted
And tried to distract her
Until our turn finally came.
We were ushered in by a friendly attendant
And led down a row of dogs in cages.
My heart was broken at their plight
And I could not look them in the eye
Until a small beige and white dog
Came bounding to the front.
Wagging her tail.
Wildly enthusiastic.

Very feminine.
Full of life. About eight months old.
We were impressed.
She was still wagging her tail when we left the room
To go to the next
Where more dogs were on view.
We saw a black spaniel-like dog
We both liked.
We almost decided
Until we remembered
The one with the waggily tail.
We went back for another look.
She was standing at the front of the cage
Watching for us.
Wagging her tail
Four-forty.
We called her Daisy.
It was Sept. 1, 1981.

DAPHNE

I met her at work.
She was much older than I.
She came from a different culture.
We became friends.
She was sophisticated
A woman of the world.
My Lady from Shanghai.
My example for
Manners, fashion, hostess.
Above all, friend.
Still my friend.
By my side
A guide.

DEAR OLD BILL

It is your birthday today
And the memory of your
Dear face has come to me
Throughout the day
Bringing a tear to my eye.
How we loved you
Beloved friend from childhood
How we love you still
That twinkle in your eye
The sweetness of your smile
You taught us there need be
No generation gap
Between old and young friends
Spending time together.
You never retired.
Just kept going
Taking care of business
Until that winter day
When by your side
We quietly said good-bye.
Four decades have passed
But the warmth of your love
Reaches down from above
As I visit with you again in spirit.

DEBTS

So many kinds
She mused.
A material girl
She thought first
Of financial debt
A companion she knew well
Who dragged her down.
She'd experienced the
Power of economic dominance
Over another
And then
Over her.
Some imbalances made better
By coin without price
The exchange made right.
Or repaid in full
As required by law
Equally right.
But debts must be paid
Whatever they be
Whatever the way
If we would be free.

DEDICATED TO ANNE MCMANUS

Once there was a princess
Her name was Margaret Anne
Now she lives in old New York
But home is Ireland.

Her hair is black and like a mane
Her eyes are made of blue
Of course she has some freckles
On skin that's clear and fair
A carriage that is straight and proud
A beauty anywhere.

But more than that
She has a heart
That Raggedy Ann would admire
Like hers it says "I Love You"
But it's not made of candy
It's made of tears and laughter
And beats stronger every day
To heal a world that needs her
Where money is not the pay.

But rich she is
Where the records are
And some day a check will be drawn
By heaven itself on heaven's bank
For Margaret of Ireland.

DINNER AT DAPHNE'S

A voyage on the ship of souls

Cast out, forsaken

They searched for a lifeline
To save them from the terror
Of themselves

This unmotley assortment of not-quite
Survivors.

Drowning, they'd found each other
And forged a raft for mutual
Protection.

Without even a paddle.

It made it easier to die.

Afraid but not alone, they thought.
They thought.

DIVINITY

Everything can be changed
Even death and taxes.

I create my own world
Concept by concept
Choice by choice
Projection by projection.
My perception of reality
Made manifest so.

If my creations
Serve not only me
But those who follow
It will be truth for me.
My own divinity.

DIVORCE

Embattled
Surrounded
She put up a fight
Hurt to the quick
But emboldened by right
Against superior might.
And so she prevailed
Over hate
Grounded in knowing
To conquer
One's fate
Be ready to meet her
Even embrace.

DOGS OR CATS?

Which do you prefer
Dogs
Or
Cats?
I dreaded the question.
I knew someday
Someone would ask.
And I could never decide.
This week, cats
That week, dogs.
A dog could dissolve me
For days
Then I would tire
Of his demand
For attention
Or
My need to give it.
Then
A cool cat
I purred for.

THE DOORMAN

He probably knows
More secrets about you
Than your banker
Or hairdresser
You need him.
A great equalizer
The doorman.
More important
Than the Super
Reserved for big issues.
One had her favorites
One spoiled more
An indispensible representative
At the front door.

DUBLIN CITY

I felt compelled to go
A ritual visit
To a beloved city
I wanted to know more.

Christmastime in Dublin
The landmarked
Hotel Gresham's
Old world charms
Coffee in the lounge
Surrounded by Christmas.
I stepped out onto
O'Connell Street
And sought the GPO
Where those who sought
Irish freedom
Died to make it so.
I entered its portals
Once again
Its majesty intact
Christmas in the General Post Office
Stopped me in my tracks.
A splendid time
To visit
Happy to be back.

A walk across the Liffy
On the Ha-penny Bridge
To wander Temple Bar
Dublin's Greenwich Village
For this I'd come afar.
To Grafton Street
Shopping
And St. Stephen's Green
Primroses in December
Can this be a dream?

A grand city tour
Spread over days
Renewing acquaintance
And learning new ways.
The Old Guinness Brewery
The view from the top
Lunch and a Guinness
One shouldn't miss
This stop.
Or its special gift shop.
The tea shoppe.
Bewley's. Scones. Sausage rolls.
A real Irish fry-up.
No diet should miss
The tastes of Ireland
I savored with bliss.

The Writers Museum
I walked it alone
Close to those now

Enshrined here in rooms
Of their own.
The glory of their words
From the living of their lives
Permeated mine.
They were not just observers of life
They chose to experience life
In its fullness.
And paid the price.
It was sometimes high,
But they were rich in spirit
If not wealth.

Words shared with us all
That have continued to live.
Hallowed rooms.
I felt blessed
At the gentle welcome.
Dublin City.

DYING

She was dying.
I knew it
I believe she did, too.
Not quite consciously
But almost.
Life had become too much trouble.
No longer convenient
Not just for those
Around her
But herself.
She wasn't there yet
There were still small pleasures.
Actually big pleasures for her
That's what it had come to
What was still important.
Money always had been
And now gave her confidence.
It brought respect
And comforts.
Independence still.
She asked for no more.
But her identity.
She kept it until the end
Aided by her partner.
Who knew.
And cared.

EARTH PLANET

Many today
Are proclaiming their divinity.
While true
This is a physical planet
Probably a rarity in the universe
For which many hunger
To have the experience.
A physical life
With all its senses
Not available to spirit.
While we who have it
Do not savor it
For its privilege.
To feel
Even grief
Is to know
We can find joy.
Grief is universal
And very personal
But grief unites
As in the tsunami
Or Katrina
Hurricanes Irene and Sandy
Makes us one in grief.

THE EASTER BUNNY

I saw the Easter Bunny
The morn before the day
When he'd be honored o'er the earth
Where young in heart held sway
He hadn't changed a bit from when
With sleepy eyes we saw
Him sitting on the window sill
Outside the bedroom door
Long years have gone since childhood
But never an Easter comes
Nor ever a bunny I see
That the wonder of the window sill
Returns in memory.

EASTER VISIT

With the first strength of morning
I saw thee for Him
The Spirit of the Mother
Arose from the mist
In changing faces from many times
But ever the same
One Mother.
We talked as Mothers do
On any plane
Of sons of any time
Who met their fondest hopes and faith
That they would live again
We whispered softly in the night
Not speaking lest we miss
The sweet soft sound of sleeping
And know that rest is His.

EIGHTY-ONE AND COUNTING

Our birthday
What did she
Think about it
Really?
Well, I remember
My Mother said:
It was the beginning
Of noticeable decline.
And she'd begun to
Notice there was
Something to this.
Preparation, she expected
For a new life
Down the road
Not yet.
Not now
Still down the road
With time to say goodbye.

EIRE

I found I could
Travel back
Quite literally
To those wonderful times
We shared
In Ireland.
One had to make time
To linger again
Along the lanes
We knew
The branches and hedgerows
Enveloping the car
As we rode
Into a day on the road.
Little villages
General shoppe and pub
Both favorites to visit
Sometimes a bakery/coffee bar
Homemade bread and jam
Sausages
An Irish coffee
Thick with cream
At the Old Gresham.
Dublin.
Sorrow and joy
Always mingled
The past with now
The GPO called to me
Rebellion against tyranny.

Worth dying for.
What, she thought,
Is there today
To compare
To die for?
Not Iraq, a cause not just,
We would not do again.

You go next time
I said.
You who sent us there
You believe.
Then go. You cannot believe
And not go
Or it becomes a lie.

EMPATHY

It is empathy
That creates the unity
Needed for peace.
Compassion for those
With whom we disagree
Allows us to be friends
Respecting our differences
While not understanding them.
Viewed dispassionately
Without violence
Or judgment
We accept diversity
The rights of others
As equal to our own
In wanting to be free.

THE EXTRA MILE

There is no traffic on the extra mile.
Been there
Have you?
Then you know
It's an uphill climb
But worth the climb
For the view.
The forever view.

FALL

Surrounded by lilacs
Astride the stone wall
These first days of autumn
The season did call
To admire the new look
She'd donned for the fall.
To be here.
To see it.
To walk it.
To be it.
The pale yellow sun
Made us all into one.
The crickets.
The bees.
The asters.
And weeds.
A dried black-eyed Susan
A rose bush in seed.
Heaven need not
Be better than these.

THE FAN CLUB

Her fan club was
In heaven
She saw them gathered round
Looking on proudly
On what was going on
On the ground.

I want you all to be
Part of it, she thought,
Because of course you are
In a seamless tapestry
That stretches far and wide
She felt their love
Across the skies
And bowed in gratitude.

THE FARM

I went back to
The farm today.
Place of much content.
A cool morning
A Franklin stove
Warmed me in August.
Birdseed was put out
For the finches.
We watched from
The kitchen table
Lots of them
Pecking from the feeder.
To share breakfast
With these little friends
A happy occasion
That began
Another day in rural Vermont.
No computer
No blog
No Facebook
No MySpace.
Peace.

FEAR

She'd put fear in
Its place at last
A comfort this should be
She herself was not so sure
Fear would let her be.
Let's be friends
She whispered
Lonely you must be
Fear shed a tear
Such folly
To be afraid of me.
But she was not so taken in
As once she might have been
She wanted proof from
Fear itself
It would improve its company.
Life will be the evidence
As only it can tell
All you've heard
And all you've seen
Will surely make it well.

FEELINGS

There's a miracle in every feeling.
Anger. Joy. Resentment. Love.
Hear them.
Listen when they come.
Do not send feelings away.
Feel them.
Honor them.
Learn from them.
Change can only happen
On a personal level
Then the collective
Is affected.
There's a miracle in every feeling.
You can change the world
Your world.
You know what to do.
All the answers are within you.
There's a miracle in every feeling.

FOR DOROTHY

The decade passed swiftly
Since you left us
Your birthday today.
You would have been 80.
Time did not heal the wound.
We are 78 now.
We keep you with us always
Tight in our hearts
And minds
As time goes on
Without you here
But never gone away.

FOR GEORGIA
(April 7)

Your spontaneity
Generosity
Creativity
Spirituality and
Adventurous spirit
Are qualities
We have enjoyed
And which we
Celebrate today
On your birthday.

FOR TWINS
 (For Rose)

It was
Our day
The one
We shared
Together.
A long time
Ago
And many times
Since.
All too few.
But life
Is eternal
And whither
I go
With me will you
Be
Because
Always
And ever
You are part of me.

FORGIVENESS

Forgiveness.
You are hard to know
Only by forgiving
Can one be in the know

Forgiveness is the antidote for alienation
From one another
It's better to be happy than right
She knew
So she chose forgiveness.

FORSYTHIA

The March sun
Shone on the bushes
Of forsythia.
Harbinger of spring
Outside my window
But not this year
No little green leaves
Peeking out
Before coming out.
No delicate yellow blossoms
Of spring.
Killed by a scaffold
For securing the terraces above
But shutting out the light
Below.
We'll replant when it's over
I'm told.
But
Will it be forsythia?

A GLIMPSE OF HEAVEN

I know how I'll know Jesus
Because I know him now
But how will I know it is Moses
When I hear them call his name?
Will I be sure in heaven
That there is only one of each?
Or will I wonder much like now
Is safety every reached?

And Jesus answered softly
In words of morning cheer.
I'll point him out to you my dear
So you can be quite sure
That this is the Moses
Of Old Testament lore.
And that this place called heaven
Is as you dreamed before.

GOING GOING GONE

With you I don't need to forget
There is nothing to remember
Except the button to be pressed
Whenever I surrender
And play the record of our love
Down rivers of my mind
In awe of my naiveté
In thinking you were mine.
There was no other woman
There was no other man
But life to live
And life to give
In necessary pain
In growing up together
But finally let's be done
With bitterness from yesteryears
Going going gone.

GOOD FRIDAY

She awoke hearing the refrain
"The story of my life
Begins and ends with You."
Over and over it played
Until she became alert to the words.

I won't do any chores today, she thought.
It's a holiday, right?

It wasn't a holiday for Jesus
Came the reply.

She was stricken at the scene
That flashed across her mind.
So old. So now.
Carrying His cross up a hill.
A crown of thorns
Nails hammered into His hands and feet.
The cross raised high.
Denied by His followers.
Abandoned by His Father
A drink of vinegar
A sword thrust.

Because He said
I and the Father are one.
And you, too, can be.
The way of the cross leads home.

She'd walked that way, too
In her own life
Searching for the straight path
The narrow one
That leads to life
Until it found her.

The journey each of us takes alone.
Different for each but the same

They met again
On the other side of the cross.
He put His arm around her.
Her head on his chest.

"The story of my life," she whispered to Him
"Begins and ends with You."

It was indeed a holiday.

GRANDMAS

I haven't been a grandma,
So I wouldn't know
What I'd do
But when I heard
What one had done
I knew what must be true.
That true did not matter
He only had to ask
For grandma to run
To rescue him and his
From all that had come to pass
Because she was his grandma
And would be to the last.

GRIEF

It was not an acquaintance of choice.
It came unbidden
To claim my attention.

And got it.

I wasn't expecting the reality it was
Different for each.
It was so many things.
So many shared memories
Play on the record of the soul
Embedding themselves forever
Becoming part of the whole.

Never welcome, Grief.
But it can be changed into gold
A process known of old
Alchemy for new life
That only Grief unfolds.

GROWING OLD

It was happening now
To her.
She'd heard about it
Read about it
Seen it, of course.
Participated even
Within her own family.
But now it had arrived for her.

She was growing old.
Sixty-five
Is the end of middle age, she mused.
And it was just over the horizon.

She couldn't wait
For all the freedoms it would bring.
She envisioned the next 20 years
As something like the first 20
With the difference of discrimination
That 45 years in-between had wrought.
With its promise of harvest
And new fields to plant
Before winter.

GUILT

She knew what she had done.
It was crazy.
She felt bad about it
For years.
It could not be undone.
It could not be confessed.
More harm than good.
Became a regret
For her to bear alone.
How could she atone
She asked?
Forgive was the reply.
Forgiven came the word.

HALLEY

She was our "native-born-Vah-man-tah,"
The very essence of what Vermonters
Mean to us flatlanders
Who arrived only three decades ago.
She was our role model
The one who fulfilled
The image we held –
Who made it reality
For three generations of our family.

Always our first visit
On a trip to Vermont
Was to her house.
Often for home-baked donuts
Like none other
In her cozy kitchen
Over coffee
Catching up on family and local news;
Or for maple syrup on snow
As she stirred long the pot
While we waited and watched
For the syrup to get hot.

Then a yard tour to see
What was blooming.
Pansies by the door.
Geraniums overflowing pots
Hollyhocks and morning glories
The wash blowing in the wind.

The vegetable garden
Whose produce frequently
Graced our table
Through her generosity.

We walked her fields
Exhilarated by the views
Of meadows filled with daisies.
The green mountains
In changing seasons.

We sat by her campfire
In the woods
On summer evenings
Over lavish picnics
Under the stars.
The aroma of hot dogs
And roasted corn
Homemade salads and relish
Lots of beer
Family and neighbors
Gathering here.
Unforgettable memories
Of one we hold dear
Unforgettable memories, Halley,
To keep o'er the years.

A HANDSHAKE OR A KISS

It seemed to her
A handshake was
More meaningful
A firm clasp
Eye to eye contact
A smile.
While most kisses
Airbrushed.
Not always of course
But a peck on the cheek
Even a hug
Not as sleek
As hand to hand
Eye to eye
That meet.

HEATHER HILLS IN IRELAND
(For Mother, 9/27/81)

I

A warm September day
The sun on our backs
As we climbed "The Vee"
With the Mother of me.
She stopped for crystals on the way
Sprigs of heather were her first bouquet
On her visit to Ireland
One late summer day.

II

Rams munched on the hillsides
Immobile in heather
A painting by nature
Of its wooly creature
Engraved in my mind
As though hung on the wall
For memory to bring back
When e'er I recall –
The steep mountain climb
With the stone grave atop
The view across counties
And all of our steps.

III

The gardens at Lismore
That we did not see
Impressive Mount Melleray
And its monastery.
Tea at Knocklofty
And a walk by the Suir
Through gardens of flowers
Round the house of Dunmore.
A day in the country
At the time of full moon.

Heather hills in late bloom.
Heather hills in late bloom.

HEAVEN

She felt that heaven was closer now
The veil between dimensions clearer
And thought she saw why
The veil parted by loved ones
Gone before
Making it easier to die.
Knowing death
Takes only bodies
Not our souls
Which are as close
As we want them to be
As love brings
Their spirits near
To walk and
Whisper with us here.

HEAVEN HERE

What if I told you that, actually,
Heaven is here?
You have to create it yourself, mind you
Your own design.
It's your time here
To do with
What you will
Your choices.
It's hard to make good choices
Among all there is
Because the choices themselves can be hard
Involving hard work to bring dreams to life
Stone cutter work
But clean and pure
With help along the way.
Spiritual citations
In the ether
Cosmic awards
That carry us forward.

HEAVEN ON EARTH

What would you like
Your heaven to be?
Why not make it now?
What pleasures are your favorites
Are these within your grasp
Build them brick by brick
Into a life
Only you ask.
It would reflect
The one you know best
No one else comes close
You know yourself far better
Than those who like you most.
And so her days were spent
Creating a heaven here
Just as she would like it.
This was easier said than done
But a goal well worth
The striving.

HEIDI ... A MOUNTAN GOAT

Heidi was a naughty goat
Continually in trouble
She worried Peter very much
Because she always strayed
From the path he'd picked with care
To graze that warm spring day.

While all the others romped and played
In meadows bright with daisies
Heidi wandered farther on
Because she heard a song
That sang to her that higher up
Were flowers never seen
That she would see for Peter
And those who would not come.

So Heidi scrambled upward
'Til all the trees were gone
And only rocks and crevices remained
Before the summit.
She didn't find any flowers
Her knees were scratched and sore
She'd never been so high
Was terrified she'd fall.

Exhausted she lay in a cleft of the rock
And looked at the cliff to the summit
No rocks ... just small footholds
Were the steps that led to the top

Heidi knew she couldn't make it
Except perhaps by a leap
And she was too tired to try,
To look down now made her dizzy
And finally she started to cry.

It was how Peter found her
Cradled between two rocks.
He pushed her ahead to the summit
And told her not to look down
That he was in back and would catch her
To keep her eyes on the crown.

It was still at the top of the mountain
Heidi had never seen such a view
Or been up so late to catch sight
Of a red sky at night.

Peter led them down the mountain's other side
A gently winding trail to home.

HENRY

How oft have I thought of you
Down through the years
Wondering what it was
What hold in fascination
Your memory still invokes.
I've never solved that mystery
Except to know for sure
The power of your person
Is one that will endure.

I asked Rose one day
How she felt about Henry?
I don't like him, she said.
In fact, I hate him.

My heart faltered within.
I didn't understand why I didn't hate him, too.
I wanted to. Tried to. But couldn't.

It's true he was odd.
Or was he?

I never really did believe
It was more than a put-on.
A clever subterfuge
To hide a mind that saw
How little chance he had to share
A love his brother'd won
Because he was the image
Of a Grandpa close to home.

And so in time turned inward
To gradually become
In life as mad
As he'd made up
Believing we become.

HERE'S TO COMEDIANS

Who leave a
Legacy of laughter.
Thinking of Alan Sherman
Whose humor I loved
His recordings
Remembered with a chuckle
Sometimes close to tears.
His humor spanned decades
The same ones as mine
Contemporaries.
Heaven has more joy now
Alan is there
Joined by another Alan this week.
Alan King.
Here's to comedians.

HIZZONER THE HERO
(September, 2001)

The mayor of New York
Took command of his city
Marshaled his forces
To search and recover
The missing and lost.
Visited the wounded
Loved ones in shock
Rallied New Yorkers
To how we could help
Blood, volunteerism
Time and supplies
Shelter and money
For those still alive
Fearless, he showed us
What we, too, must be
Able and ready
To defend liberty.
Rudolph Giuliani
Like Churchill they said
A baseball cap on his head.

Rudy
Everywhere
Praising, exhorting, explaining.

Now we must feel
Take time to heal
For freedom over fear
For hatred
God Allah forgive us
For not seeing
For not helping
Them
To understand us
Or us them
So we would not
Do this
To each other again
But live in love
And peace.

A great outpouring of love
Has been showered
Upon our city, New York
It bathes us in its light
And wipes away our tears.

HOSTAGE

You are free, he said.
My mind tried to take it in.
Was it real? Or a new cruelty?
I was too frightened to believe
Though I desperately wanted to.
I waited without breathing
To hear more.
There were details.
I listened warily.
Having experienced for so long
Man's inhumanity to man.
Firsthand.

Forgive me, he said,
It was never personal you know
Good luck and all that
And on with the show.
I had been rescued.
Brought back by my country.
With prayers and diplomacy.

My Country 'Tis of Thee.

HOW SWEET IT IS

The moment.
If only she
Could stay
In that frequency
Draw it out
See its depth
And width
And height
How unseen the moment
In all that it was
Show me
Show me
All that you are.

I DON'T HAVE TO KNOW

I don't have to know
When?
How?
What? Why?
Whatever. I believe.
I believe
It hangs together
I know not how
What does it matter
Why waste time
Asking why
Believe in the universe
Do not deny
The Force that has manifest
Give it a try.

I HAVE CHOSEN YOU
(By Timmie McManus, Age 9 days)

I hope you like surprises
'Cause I have one for you
I may seem small and speechless
But really I am not
If you listen carefully
I speak from heart to heart
I chose you 'cause you're special
And I want more for you
Than all the dreams you've dreamed for you
For Adam or for John
It is here that we'll begin
As God on earth is born again.

THE INTERNET ROMANCE

They didn't meet on the internet
But it kept them connected.
They hadn't known it would
Until work
And then romance
Motivated them
To make friends
With their computers.
Their skills improved
With practice.
The pleasure of instant gratification
A subject of
Unfair repute
Was theirs.
The internet,
A romantic place.

INTERPLANETARY CONNECTIONS

She felt it happen
She had made an
Interplanetary Connection.

Meditation brought her there.
She was a little frightened
At first
Where does one go
When the chips are up?
Home, of course.

She went.
At the speed of light
To safety.
She had the armor of 73 years.

She felt strange
Surrounded as she was
By surrender.

The Surrender Ceremony
Allows
Access to the archives.
To bow the spirit
Is to become one
With all
And all is ours
Words are real.
Be careful with them.

IRELAND

Take me there
Oh, take me there
Again.
How she loved it
The hedges
Winding roads
Walls covered with nasturtiums
The view over the hills
To Slievenamon
The woodpile
Where the cat slept
Hidden from near view
Dew on the morn
Lilacs in bloom
Thank you for heaven
She breathed
To not see it
Is not to know
That it can be had
Here and now.

IRISH SPRING

I'd come home
As they say
In the month of May
After 17 years.
The fields were a
Brilliant green dotted
White and yellow.
Daisies and
Buttercups
The hedgerows lush
With gorse
Lilacs bloomed
Over stone walls
And the Blackthorne tree
Both white and pink
Was a feast for the eyes
And soul.

IT'S GONE

A life she knew for years
Gone in an instant
It hadn't even happened yet
But she missed it already.
She saw it arriving.
Had sometimes wished for it
Suddenly she knew
How much it meant to her
There was still time to
Make it count
She redoubled her efforts
To make heaven on earth.
Create it now
The happiness she willed
For the time remaining
To be remembered until
We would meet again
And reminisce.
Moon River.

JOANNE
(For Rose)

She had flaming red hair
And a temper to match.
We knew one another from kindergarten
And were friends until the end
Seventy years later.

She was a party girl
In a time when smoking was seductive.
Even romantic.
A beer drinker to excess
Joanne never did anything halfway.

Pretty and vivacious
Men were attracted
And caused jealous rages in her marriage.

Her only child – Charlie – died at 16
In a bike accident with a drunk driver.

She never recovered.
She went through the motions of life
Tending her lovely garden and home.
Her spirit broken
Her marriage in tatters.

She lunged into binge drinking
Lit one cigarette from another.
Two good friends stood by.

Her husband died
And she knew some peace.

But a lifetime of excess caught up
She did not die alone.
Rose was at her hospital bedside in Florida.

She loved jewelry, but only the real thing.
I wear a ring of hers, as does Rose.
So, she is still with us,
Reminding us of her love of life
And spirit of adventure.
The good times we shared.

She was on our minds this week.
Trying to reach us, I thought
To tell us something.

Perhaps that she and Charlie
Were together again
In a new place.
I like to think so.

We love you, Joanne.

JOHNNY

Here's Johnny!
It was a unifying death
The nation mourned
An icon of television comedy
Johnny Carson.
He ruled the night air
For three decades
Undisputed emperor.
Left today
Sunday, the 23rd of January.
Born in Iowa the 23rd of October 1925.
Raised in Nebraska
A Midwesterner.
Came to Malibu.
Dead of emphysema at 79.
Sorely missed
Since retirement
At 67.
When he left the stage
Not to return
Until today.
His chosen epitaph:
"I'll be back."

JOSEPHINE

Ah, but he could never conquer Josephine
No, he reflected, he could not!
When she was the belle of Paris
He was forgiving.
When she was barren for fourteen years
He could not
And divorced her.
She retired to their summer home
Where he thought of her often.

A JOURNEY

I

Anywhere in time
I wanted to roam
The desire grew
And emboldened the wish
It took a leap forward.

II

A happy scene. Make me a happy scene.

Give me the courage to be happy.

Let it be so.

Why didn't someone tell me it took so much courage to be happy?

Ah, so it is again as many sacred subjects.
It could not be told.
The way was too long, the path too steep to be borne before
The joy of arrival swept away the memory of the journey.

III

But I did not forget.
Would not
Could not
Should not.

I will remember the way
Until I am the way
So happiness need ne'er be lost again.

JUNIE

She was our childhood friend.
Schoolmate.
She came into our classroom one day.
A new girl. Eugenia.
Of Ukrainian ancestry, we were told.
We were impressed by this news.
And her strange name
We called her Junie.

Then we learned that she lived
Just down the road
At the corner atop the hill
Facing High Mountain.
We visited often.
Became best friends.
Tomboys, we explored the neighborhood
Within a radius of two miles.
Had many adventures.
Sometimes we got caught.
And were banished from playing together
For a time.
Her father would say:
"She has to practice piano."

I remember the kitchen
Her mother at the sink
Making dinner.
Her father in the field.
We came to know him better.

We liked to hear them talk.
Their accents
He seemed to work all the time.
We never saw him idle.

He had a quiet way.
A warm smile.
Just as Junie did.
She didn't go to our high school.
But to a private one.
We were sad about that.

Our lives drifted apart.
In the decades that followed.
We saw one another infrequently,
But with the easy way of old friends.

Then in the next generation
Son Paul continued
The friendship
With my mother.
By helping about the yard.

She was very fond of him.
He called her "Grandma."
He brought us the news about you.
It hurt. So young. So bright.
So responsible.
Her work done
In the school of life.
We don't need to see her
To have her with us in spirit.
As close as a thought
Keeps her memory alive.

KNOWING HELL

To really know hell
You have to go there
Some of us go more than once.
Drawing near to the fire
Until an ocean comes to the rescue.
It's easier to recognize heaven
When you've been to hell.

I reached for the star that I am
Didn't Bright Star say so?
"I am a star.
A star is a heavenly body radiating light.
I am a heavenly body radiating light.
I am a star."
Do not think
Just do
Trusting
In your perfection
Believing in yourself
Help me to astonish them
Tut tut
Always competitive.

LABOR DAY 1980
(*Central Park A Visit With*
Hans Christian Andersen)

Sitting on the park bench
Trying to de-stress
I was startled to see
The statue of the fairy tale teller
Was tired and drawn.
From what I wondered?
I thought you were in paradise.
No rest there, I reflected
And gazed over
At the lake where
Sailboats idled in the 90 degree sun
Suddenly a tiny yellow and black craft sped
Through the water defying the heat.
A happy boat.
It was so insouciant that I laughed
And turning saw the statue
In a different light – no longer tired.
Several children leaned on his breast
While one read aloud the stone story of the
Ugly Duckling.
And then as visitors changed
Hans's visage and pose did too.
He seemed to have a special light for some.
And I meditated on this phenomenon.

LAST WILL AND TESTAMENT
(From John to Stella)

I had a wonderful Easter
The best ever
In some ways
In others,
Decidedly not.
It will be my last
Here
But a part of me
Will be yours always
To add to the
Wonderful you
Who has given me
So much.
It's all I have to give, really.
Myself.
I leave myself to you
My darling Stella.

LEGACIES

I did not have to wait for her to die
To get a legacy.
She gave freely of herself and what she had
While we were both alive
When most I needed some of both
Her spirit and her purse were open wide.
No matter other legacies
No matter what their size
There's none I'll treasure more than these
From friendship at my side.

∽

The next dimension
Is a network
Of spirits known to us through history
Petals of their achievements in consciousness
Flow back as blessings to the earth
And raise the spirits of those to whom
They are revealed
In luminescence.
In a twinkling of an eternal eye.

A LETTER TO HEAVEN

Dear Dorothy,

Rose and I have come to Vermont for the restoration being here always brings and to be close to your spirit on the land you loved and made yours.

Your new lilac bush by the barn is in bloom. Two purple iris are out, and the daffodils on the bank above the pump still here. The kitchen perennial garden under the apple tree is outrageously glorious, and it has been a special gift to see its tall yellow and purple tulips, primroses, white violets, bleeding hearts and other floral harbingers of spring beneath the apple blossoms.

Your day lilies around the pond in the meadow are doing well and there are at least 30 goldfish from the pair with which you began.

We've had asparagus from the garden, and I've made rhubarb twice – a cobbler and stewed.

Charles went to Lebanon today to get a cap for his new Ford green pickup. There's a bluebird in the bluebird house, goldfinches galore, and humming birds on the porch.

Everything we do reminds us of you.

Much love,
Evelyn

LIFT-OFF
(Ode to Columbia Space Shuttle Mission III Launch)

Sunlight above
Lift-off below
The count down in time
Until all systems go.
The orbiter is ready
To wing toward the sky
Test flight for America
In learning to fly
On frontiers of space
Where few men have gone
Exploring the air
Whence cometh the light
To study the Sun
The planets in flight
To bring back the news
And photos from space
To accelerate brotherhood
In advancing the race.

We salute you, Columbia
On behalf of the Earth
Land of our birth.

T-minus 1
Counting
T-minus 50 seconds
On-board computers
Sequence on orbiter

Ignition.
Main engine ignition
Lift-off! Lift-off!

LIMITED PARTNERSHIP

Birds fluttering down the tree
A cascade of birds
Falling from above.
In formation
An elaborate design
Down near the ground
Then up again
Soar
To the treetop.

Aging makes us
See it better
Enjoy it more
Because soon it will be gone
A brief moment
In the sun
And then
We will be done.

A LINE AT A TIME

Every time I write a poem
I have a vision
It unfolds
Line by line
None of them
Ahead of time.
The experience
Like life itself
Comes
A line at a time.
A moment in time.
Unhurried.
'Tis mine.

LINGER

Linger awhile
This last day of the year
And think about you.

I know myself better.
I accept myself more.
I am kinder to myself.
I am more balanced.
I am more centered.
I am more aware of my dark side and how to
Love it into integration.
I am learning to pace myself better.
I am taking more responsibility for my decisions or not.
I am more conscious of choices.
I am more conscious.
I am more self-aware.
I am more confident.
In my authentic presence of being.

And for next year.
More of all of the above, please.

LOVES

Many loves had she.
Some more important than others.
Some more physical
Others of the heart
Others spiritual
Others friendship
The happiest.

LUCK

I'd rather be lucky than good
It's been said.

Really, she responded.
Like a lucky thief? Serial killer? Abuser? Cruel? Thoughtless?
Unkind?
No virtues.
But lucky. Not good.

I suppose if one were any of these
It would be great to be lucky.

She believed in luck.
Earned luck.
Called synchronicity.
Perfect timing in the flow of life.
A gift from the universe
For being good.

Earned luck.

MADE IN VERMONT

We saw it first at the Tunbridge flea market
My sister Dorothy and I.
A raccoon against a painted winter scene
Of holly and evergreen on muslin
Encased in a wood embroidery hoop
Surrounded by lace.
Eight dollars it was
Too much, we decided
Next day we saw another
In Ben Franklin's window
In Randolph
This time in green and red hoops
Accompanied by a bunny, squirrel and goose.
We rushed inside
And bought the fixings for
A bunny, raccoon and goose
For just under $10.
We were proud of our bargain.
It seemed simple enough
Even though I hadn't embroidered
For more than 40 years.

Dorothy had outlined the bunny and goose
While I was stitching laboriously on Max, the raccoon.
Then we improved upon the original
By stuffing ours
Until they were raised and plump.
We added muslin backing to hide the stitches.
It was then our craft fun turned complex.

Round and round Dorothy sewed
On the old treadle machine
Adding the lace. Three dollars more.
It was too fat to fit inside the hoop.
We pulled at the lace
Squeezed, pressed and held
But no way could we get
The hoop to stay firm.
We cut more and made worse
'Til at last we gave up
'Twould be a potholder, bread basket
Or pincushion, we said.
We stuffed the whole thing
A pillow did make
The hoop it went on
And we moved on ahead.
The goose she came next,
A near thing it was
But practice makes perfect
She really looked great.
Max the raccoon
Was the last and the best.
Except for the loops
To hang them, she said.
En fin, on the way
Looking just grand
We admired our presents
The work of our hands.

MAGGIE

Once she was Maggie.
It was long ago
But now and then
She would return.
Her face I would see
Behind mine
In the mirror
And I remembered
Where it was
In Eire.
A cottage
A garden
An old stone wall
Where we would meet
And pledge our love
A love that could
Not be
But would some day
In a world yet to come
Together again.

MANAGEMENT BY OBJECTIVE

Corporate language
She'd learned
By doing it.
Plan the year ahead
Outline your goals
For each area
Of responsibility
Check your progress
Along the year
To the day of accountability.

A measure she now used
Daily.
The structure of her day.
Make a list of
Must do's
Want to do
Any fun today?

She let the order
Set itself
Left space
For spontaneity
Some things she
Thought important
Time did not allow
And sometimes added others.
But it was the structure
The architecture of her life

The progress of its building
That gave her
The satisfaction
Her soul required
For peace.

MANHATTAN SNOWFALL

We walked through the falling snow
On East 81st Street.
Christmas lights twinkled
Along a festooned fence
And a wreath sparkled
On a townhouse door.
A lovely scene
I shared with my cancer-stricken friend
Just after a radiation treatment.

Now on our way to the Met
Rather a long crosstown walk
But she insisted
On the exercise.

We had some lunch at the Museum
And then visited the Scythian Gold Stag exhibit.
She had in mind the purchase of a Stag with antlers high
Wood covered with gold plate.
She decided to wait
Until radiation test results were in.

We sat for a time
As exhaustion and some disorientation
Overwhelmed her.
She often pushed herself too far.

The snow was still falling
As we left.
She finally agreed to take the crosstown bus
To Lexington and then another bus
Down to her apartment on 54th.

I left her there at 79th & 5th Avenue
A frail but determined figure
Living while dying her way.

MARION

Memories of Marion
Played on the screen
Culled from the canvas
Anew to be seen
Through the eye of the poet
Who sees
The musician.
The mother.
The friend.

She was my friend's mother.
My friend, too.
She fulfilled my idea of a lady.
A genteel lady.
She reminded me of other times.
Softer times.
She had a pastel aura.

She was a bridge for me
Back to the twenties and early thirties
Paris.
Where she had lived a Bohemian musician's life
With an Italian painter.
A romantic time
Across the sea.

I see her later
Standing in a large hall
In a Victorian house

On a rainy afternoon
In London.
Sipping sherry
By the fire
Playing the piano
For a small gathering
Of intimate friends
On a country weekend.

She loved London
And lived there again
For a year
In her old age
On Shaftsbury Avenue.

In New York
She lived in a Greenwich Village
Brownstone
Where we often visited.
She played the organ
In local churches
Until she was mugged one night.
She moved to Woodstock, N.Y.
And shared a house with a friend –
Until the end.

I never pass
Bank Street
Without thinking
How much she
Missed the City
And wishing
She was there.

THE MARRIAGE

The daughter of the Master of Time
Opened her eyes
And observed with affection
Her Father's Kingdom.

She took the old brown clock in her hands
And journeyed backwards
To the time
When marriage began
Twenty-one years ago. In the spring
She remembered. It was the first day of spring.

The reels unfolded slowly
Karmically entwined
To meet again
Those partners from a former time
And reach the balance of opposites
For the freedom of my kind.

The years now seemed more gentle
Time had softened them
With wisdom from her store
To blur with love the lessons
Unknown heretofore.
To reach the bonds of marriage
Envisioned in my heart
Not knowing then that it was I
Who must bring the dream to life

By becoming the dream
And being met by a man
Whose dream was the same.

I thought that I had found him
And waited for his call
Indecision triumphed
Until the love-child, grown weary with
Impatience, called.
Destiny complete, they parted
Bonded eternally in their child.

Time stood still for long years
Until Aquarius whispered yes.
His voice was of daffodils and lilies of the valley
Lured by Uranus
She married again
And discovered her brother.
His mien was of Saturn
And the karma they sealed
Freed them forever from martyrdom's fields
And gave them the right to martyrdom's crown
Studded with diamonds of laser light
From the electric planet
That pierced the night.

Time waited with them.
Patient. Loving. Sacrificing.
Skirting fulfillment
Knowing deep within
That non-fulfillment
Was the love

Needed for the prize
That karmic debts would cancel
And love immortalize.

The planet Uranus drew nearer
Time gathered the speed of light
And the end of time was near
For the fulfillment of my image
Of marriage.

Created in time
Known in time.
Immortalized in time
To become eternal.

The daughter paused in eternity
And held the old brown clock to her heart.
And all the time it had told was hers to keep.

MARTYRDOM

She'd given up martyrdom
Downright got sick of it
Laying her life down
For a friend.
Better love hath no man
Was the word.
She'd fulfilled it
And was ready to move on.

MASTER OF TIME

I wandered through time, unknowing
Looking for myself
And here and there I found me
And then again was lost.
Time passed on
And still I searched
To learn at last
The answer was not here
But locked in space
Kept safe for me
Until I could draw near.
And understand the purpose
Of my journey to this place
To master time with power
From the infinity of space.

MAY DAYS ... A TRIP

Everywhere I turned the universe spoke with me

A kiss in the sky
A lady in black
An escort and car
A fountain and tree
Tree-starved, she said. I said, how about this? Too short and fat? Then how about that? Too tall? Nice, she said. But not mine. Mine's just not here. But I know where it is.

The men in the lobby
Appointment not kept
The money in red
The phone calls from bed.

The TV that told us
To please turn it on
The hot plate at breakfast that reached out to burn
In reply to my unspoken word.

The conference around me that dizzyingly swirled
You spoke through the sign that said, Careful Wet Floor.
It was dry, but I knew that for me it was wet
And I left when you called me to go home to bed.

I asked for the doctor to help me to sleep
He came but I wouldn't.
I wanted to watch
Though frightened and worn
The universe talk with me more.

And so you continued
Until death stood nearby
And I pushed shut the door of the sky into sleep.

ME

My way is ordered
By the stars
Ones I'd assembled
For the trip
To the new planet.
A lot of Capricorn at the top of the mountain
The Power of Fortune
In Pisces
Uranus in Ascendant Aries
Taurus intercepted in the 1st with
Gemini air 2 and 3
Jupiter in 4
With Pluto.
Mars in 5
Neptune 6
South node
In 7. Destiny in partnerships.
Scorpio between 7 and 8
Nine for Sagittarius
Moon and Venus conjunct.
Fairy Godmother.
That's me.

MEMORIES OF AUNT RUTH
(Ruth E. Howes Commerford
November 3, 1915 – December 4, 2004)

She was just a teen-ager when Rose and I were born. Sixteen. She always seemed young to us because she was fun. When we were with her, we had a good time.

We went to Short Beach and Branford Point. Savin Rock Amusement Park and Ward's Pond. A memory there she never let us forget.

It was a hot summer day. Aunt Ruth was pregnant. We three sat in the pond to cool off. Suddenly, Aunt Ruth said: "Look. There's a bloodsucker!" In a flash, Rose and I put a hand on each of her shoulders, pushed ourselves up and fled. Leaving her to drown, she said!

Sometimes we went fishing. I'll never forget the time I put my bare foot into the bait – a pail of worms. Or put a worm on a fish hook for the first time.

Aunt Ruth loved nature. As we did. Birds and flowers were among her passions. Genes that the Howes' family passed on to us. Grandpa Howes was a professional gardener. In Aunt Ruth's Connecticut garden was a small sign reflecting that love.

"A kiss of the sun for pardon
The song of a bird for mirth
We're nearer to God in a garden
Than any place else on earth."

Her spirit is with us today as she returns to her beloved New England. Branford. Where she left her heart. And now her body. Next to Uncle Fran. Together forever. As they wished.

We love you, Aunt Ruth. And thank you. We look forward to seeing you both again in that glorious garden above.

MEMORIES OF CHILE

I am in Chile
Sitting at the pool of the Hotel Sheraton.
Sunday morning.
It is lovely.
But I am numb.
Displaced geographically.
The sun is delicious
While New York is frigid.
I feel alien
Even though my Spanish
Is good.
And fools most everyone.
Thank God for Ximena
Wonderful friend.
She'll come for me at 12.
We'll go to the Jumbo *supermercado*
Then to Bebe's for lunch.
The dollar is down again
And I feel a new attitude
In the shops here.
They tried to raise
The price in dollars above what was written
In pesos and in dollars.
I said I would pay in the pesos written.
The aristocracy still worries about the stability
Of the government here
And prefers investment in dollars.
This is a very expensive hotel.
A coke is $6. So is a bottle of water.

On the street, bottled water is $1.
I can drink the local water now.
It takes time to adjust to it.
My tour went back to the USA without me.
I needed to stay longer in my beloved Chile.

MONA LISA

She disappeared before my eyes
Like she said she could
Pulled the curtains
Closed the door
And pocketed the key.
She did not know
The friend she'd found
Had keys for every door
Eyes that saw what no one else
Had ever seen before.
Mona… Mona Lisa
She said she could
And could she did.
And now we both know more.

MOTHER'S DAY

I look at you
And I see
Your Mother
Her Mother
Daddy's Mother
Grandma
A long line of Mothers
Multiplied over the planet.
A mighty force
Behind us
As you add to the legacy.
It flows on.

MT. LYMPUS

October called to me
I saw her face
Her stately form
A scene of exquisite
Aloneness; purity.
We spoke as I walked
Across the pine-ringed hill
Past the ancient apple tree
Giving birth once more
Its aged fruit a mellow hue
From memory's ancient store.
The Tree of Life upon my soul.
The land of leaves
My feet caressed
Of yellow, red and brown
The granite rock
Lavender daisies
Mushrooms in the field
Little yellow posies
The presence of the real
To meet again these sentinels
Guardians of the deep
To walk and talk together
A harvest mine to reap.

MUSICAL MEMORIES
(For Verne at 92)

He had a musical memory
Developed over decades
Of listening
While doing his homework
In the wee morning hours.
The big bands were his favorites
And stayed with him
All his long life.

There was scarcely a popular song
Whose words he did not know
Through the thirties on.
Every crooner of those times
Until the music changed
Was in his repertoire.
Lyrics for every occasion
In life
Were remembered
And shared with family and friends.
Musical memories always with him.

One of the pleasures without price
That still accompany his days.
Like his friend, Lawrence Welk,
He keeps a song in his heart.

MY DOUBLE
(For Rose)

It's a good thing
There are two of me
She thought.
To complete
What I forgot
I'd never make it
Through this world
If a twin I was not.
How do others do it?
How much easier for me
How much more of life is possible
With a double there
Thought she.
It has been true
My whole life through
Double the pleasure and pain
With one from the start
Who helped play my part.
Without whom
I would not be.

MY ROOM

She looked about
At her surroundings
Earthly pleasures.
Books, lamps, art,
Most from family and friends.
And lovers.
Surrounded by history.
Hers.
It's come out cozy
She reflected.
Warm in her room's embrace.

MY SISTER'S GARDEN

Granddaughter of an English gardener
Daughter of another in New Jersey
Dorothy made her own
In her backyard
In Davis, California.
It was hard here
With less rain
And an unrelenting summer sun
But as I sat in its triumphant midst
Enjoying its tradition of color and variety
Renewed again in my time.
This garden
Spoke of home.

NOW

To understand
To enjoy the moment
Even in a dark time
Is to understand time.

Accept it
Believe it
Relate to it
Now.

Saturn is the master clock
And always is in perfect
Time.

And as the
Night
Returns to dawn
The
Moon
Will move the tide
The flow and
Ebb
Of life
Among
The earth
The night
And times
Is a secret of the
Moon.

OCTOBER

A mellow sun
Beaming down
On my Riverside Park
Bench
Brown leaves at
My feet.
Pigeons on parade
Babies and nannies
While mothers not there
Missed out
Not knowing that
Nothing they did
Could equal the splendor
Of this autumn day.

OCTOBER 12, 2004

The nicest of days
To Chambers Street and the River
Down the esplanade
To the Irish Hunger Memorial.
Serendipity.
Walked directly into the World Financial Center
Down the new stairs
To the Palm Court below
And out to the boat basin.
The sun warmed us as we
Walked up to the 9/11 site.
A new vertical blind fence
Allows one to look down.
There are photos of the area through the years
And the re-opened World Trade Center Path Station.
A walk to Century 21
A discount store for shoppers worldwide
In business again.
My first visit.
It is huge.
I bought a red cashmere sweater
Felt I must buy something
Having come all this way.
I'll be back to explore.

We walked up Broadway
To the only place
I know to eat
Near City Hall,

Nathan Hale's
Great old pub.
We couldn't finish our drinks.
I had chicken quesadillas.
Stella, calamari and grilled veggies.
We wandered to Canal Street
And sidewalk vendors.
I bought a winter hat
And chenille scarf.
We bought fruit from a peddler
And paid a visit to a Chinese bakery.
A paradise of treats.
The M16 took us to
Park and 34th
And a last stop at
Jack's 99 cent store.
We bought rice pudding
And bread.
Walked up 52nd Street
To get the No. 5
An express bus home.
Fun day.
Remembered.

OCTOBER VISIT

Her annual visit
A clear day
A mellow sun.
I went to Central Park
Drank autumn in.
A solitary walk
Down the lilac path
The fence lush with
Morning glories
Mauve and pink
Intertwined.
I stopped
To kiss a few
Flower faces
On the fence.
A heavenly scene on earth.
She took a photo
With her heart
Always to recall
This walk
In New York's garden
This lovely day of fall.

ODE TO A BYGONE SUMMER

The air hung heavy on my soul
I felt it pierce my heart
And while I flinched before its folds
I came to claim this part
This stillness tall and deep and wide
An all-engulfing tide of October starkness
Walking by my side.
Above. Beyond. Below me
Surrounded
Bleak and gray
With a perverse fullness
That would not go away
Mist and mildew
Quiet sounds
Fall on leaves and moss
Mourning summer's passage
Nature's annual loss
Heavy now with harvest
Autumn is once more.

ODE TO THE FARM

From high on the
Rock
Near the back door
She stood
And looked out
At autumn.
Once more.
Always different
Never the same.
Never different
Always the same.
She became
Autumn too
The autumn of
Her life
Experienced anew
In a space filled
With memories
Of lives that we knew.

OD'ED ON SORROW
(For Nancy)

It was a heavy weight
To carry.
Grief so deep
Could only be
A survivor of 9/11.

She had been there.
Died with them
Yet lived
Not quite sure why
Yet.
But believing
That living well
Would be her
Tribute to them.
What they would
Have wanted
For themselves.
A second chance
To appreciate physical life.

She channeled her grief
Into living art.

THE OFFICE

I saw an office on the TV
And my heart asked for mine
Not any particular one
Just the office
All of mine
Any of mine
All of them history
At the same moment
The present.
I visited the office
Here in view
I was the boss
I was the manager
I was the secretary
It was my office
Always with me.
I took it with me.
I couldn't let it go.

OLD AGE

Something to be experienced
No one can really
Tell you
What it is like.
Because it is different
For each of us.

Old Age has changed
A lot
Recently.
Seventy is now considered
Young
By quite a few people
Who've been there lately.
And by those in their 80s and 90s.

She couldn't say she felt old.
But she was becoming acquainted
With what old age had in store
From those who are there.
Whose lives she shared.

THE OLYMPICS
(Torino 2006)

What did they mean to her?
The Olympics.
She saw the training
All consuming
What was needed
For gold.
True in all our lives
She thought.
Leadership is not easy
But it has its rewards
As all heroic efforts do
To rise above the every day
To show what we can do.
We can all be Olympians
A matter of the will.

ON BEING A TWIN

No one can know
Unless one is one
What it means
To be an identical twin.
It is shared only with one
It cannot be explained
In interviews
Or by questionnaires.
It is a mystery
Only the twins know
Can try to tell
But cannot.
It is too big
Too deep
Too wide
Too tall
It is for them
Alone.

ON RETIREMENT

Grief seized and shook her
Forced out her tears
'Til exhausted
Sleep came to help
Forget for a time
The terrible pain
She'd inflicted on herself
'Twas a comfort to know
It would all pass away
That space and time would win out
And she'd look back to then
With a smile
With a tear
On a world that came to an end.
By her own hand.
By her own tongue.

She was pleased with herself
She'd done it well, she reflected
And thought of the new world
Now forming
Within
And without.
Wow.
What a dreamer, they said
And, of course, they were right
Since dreams must be made
Like dresses, records or books
If one is to learn

That dreams are the stuff
Of which the future is built.

Her mind told her so
But her heart was of lead
Her soul in deep anguish
For what was now dead.
She gave in to sorrow
Swept over and under
Cradled gently.
Cradled gently.
Soon to be free.
Soon to be free.

OO LEE

I am Oo Lee.
You see me in your mind's eye –
A monastery in Lhasa.
It is there in the mists.
It is real.
You may enter
As you do the stones.
Join the celebrants
In early morning meditation
They welcome you.
Give you a backrest
And a robe for your legs.
You are wearing your mantle
From Stonehenge.
You are ready for a mountaintop experience.

You follow them into a light airy room
Where a porridge and a tea are waiting.
Then all have their tasks
Of their own choosing
The garden.
The cooking.
The wine.
The sewing.
The sweeping.
Visitation.
As with you.

Companionship.
It is a place you have
Always wanted to be
Now you are.
In spirit teleportation.
Your soul has travelled far.
We need such visits.
From friends like you
Who confirm our prayers for you
And your work.
Peace.
Your lifelong sensitivity
Will take a new turn –
One filled with joy
And harvest.
Do not be concerned
That you are not deserving.
You will continue
To change yourself
As the mirror of the universe
Informs you.

Your mantle will guard you
Define your space
Indoors and out.
It changes density
As needed.
You will feel it.
Be conscious of it.
You are a spiritual daughter
Of Elijah the Prophet.

He is with you.
You are one.
Come again
For spiritual refreshment
And a path made light.

AN OPEN BOOK

She was an open book
She acknowledged
So open
Hardly anyone believed it
Her innocence
Her best defense.
When innocence was gone
She had to develop
A new defense strategy
As close to innocence
As possible.

For to lose
One's illusions
Is a poor choice.

AN ORDINARY DAY

She was grateful for
An ordinary day.
Late summer
The sun mellow
A tinge of autumn.
She walked in Riverside Park
Up the Old Westside Highway
Bikers had their own path now
Seniors. Runners. Babies
Dominated the way
To the community gardens
At West 92nd Street.
Where we sat
And drank in the scene.
The garden lush
From recent rain.
Lunch on Broadway
The 104 bus home
A stop for vodka
For my upcoming train ride
To Vermont.
The apartment still
But alive with the presence
Of my roommate and me
Content with our lot.
Aging but still well
Reading. Watching afternoon TV
No worries
A time to remember

When we were together
Like this.
An ordinary day.

OUR VERMONT FARM

For 50 years we owned a farm in Vermont.
One hundred acres on a hill.
Four generations of our family
Spent springs, summers, falls.
But not winters.

It had no electricity.
In the early years, light by oil lamps.
Then gas lights.
And finally, electricity by generator.
Heat by wood and kerosene stoves.
Logs from our woods.
An outhouse on the hill
The children called "The Potty House."

Water from the pump below piped from the spring
Carried up the steep hill pail-by-pail
Until a more sophisticated system with rain barrel and gravity
Brought water indoors
For the new kitchen and bathroom.
The same system made possible a shower in the pines
Surrounded by pine trees for privacy
A granite rock floor.

In time, the house's old foundation was replaced;
Its stone wall restored.
A pond dug out of the meadow
For summer swimming
Lilies planted 'round.

Sitting at the kitchen table peeling apples from our own trees.
Making potholders. Playing board games. 500-piece puzzles. Cards.
Memories of gardens, fresh produce and flowers.
The lilacs. Birdfeeders. Maple trees lining the driveway.

Vermont life embedded within us. Ours to keep.

THE PATIENCE MEDAL

Patience was her strong game
She was pleased with it
Until it became clear
That more patience was required
Olympic patience
If she were to win gold.
She surveyed the field.
Fierce competition
But competing against herself
Was what she needed to do.
She had to reach deep
Wide. Long. High.
She yielded to patience
Its essence she sought
Do it for me
Patience, be mine.
Be me, she thought.

PATTERNS BY STELLA

She was a pattern maker
A technical designer
In the fashion industry
Her day job.
An exacting one.
Millions on the line.
She taught it to others
In fashion schools.
She saw patterns
In life, too.
And shared her art
And knowledge
So we might see the patterns, too.

PAVAROTTI

The greatest tenor
Of my generation
Died today.
September 6, 2007.
The most glorious
Of voices
Was stilled.
I reached for CDs with a sound
That heaven sent
To thrill me.
Who will forget
O Sole Mio
Or *Nessun Dorma*?
Arms wide
Handkerchief high
In friendship
And song.

PEACE IN ME

Not Peace on Earth
Is what my heart must find
Before there can begin to be
Hope for all mankind.

There is no greater enemy
I'll know no greater peril
Than those I meet within myself
The ultimate in terror.

I cannot look them in the eye,
These enemies of me
My mind recoils in fright
It turns to flee from knowing
What I'm really like.

But look I must
And see I must
Before I'll understand
What I can do to help myself
And thereby every man.

PERSISTENCE

She was the most persistent
Person I knew.
She swept over reality as
Though it didn't exist
Molded it to her liking.
Willed it to happen.
Often it did.
Others dropped along the way
Exhausted by persistence
But she pressed on.
Was it worth the candle
I wondered.
Often not to me, I knew,
But why?
Was winning so important
What difference did it make?
Perhaps if one's life at stake.
Even then I was not convinced
Life at this price
Made change look good
I'd rather be happy than right.

PESSIMISM

Don't let life defeat you.
Bring the curtain down
Pessimism drains your energy
Optimism brings health
Renew your spirit
Nature's great healer.
The sun will rise tomorrow
Babies are being born.

Problems are the price of progress.

Don't choose to be a pessimist
Look beyond
Underneath
Over
Around.

Love outweighs negativity
We build a new tomorrow.

PHILANTHROPY

Anyone can be a philanthropist
Philanthropy is personal.
One can choose to be kind.
One can choose to be merciful.
One can choose to be fair.
Or any virtue be had.

You can't give 'til you have gotten
Receive 'til you've received
It will be accordingly
As you have believed.

PISCES

How glad I was to know her
Daughter of Neptune Moon
Mystical and magical
Teacher of new tune.
Borne in on a foam-capped wave
Wrapped in violet hue
Misty water element
With special vibes for you.

Empathy is her essence
She knows just how you feel
Emotion plunging into depths
Only Pisces feel.

Mutable, flexible mermaid
Whither will you go?
Upstream ... down
All around ...
Spraying Neptune's glow.

PLATEFUL OF STRESS

She looked at her plate
A heaping one of stress

I can't eat this
She thought

Worse than fat
Worse than carbs

Stress kills.

I must transform it
At once

Into tranquility.

A visit to a friend
Whose comatose lover
Lies uptown
Problems much bigger than mine
Which can be overcome.

A walk in the park
Flowers in bloom
Butterflies on the wing
The scent of summer.
Triplets and twins on the promenade.
Lunch on Broadway
A stop at the food store.

Tranquility. Renewal.

I had turned self-pity
Into strength

By overcoming negativity.

PLAY IT AGAIN, PLEASE

Be here with me now
We who loved long ago
She could bring him back
She found
Just by letting go
Letting him enter
As the opening of a door
To make again a hologram
The way it was before.
Reality dreams
Create them sure.
You can go home again
If you insist
And insist she did
Such sweet daydreams
Memories of bygone days
To relive the scenes
Played on the record
Her heart and mind
Had made for her.
Play it again, please.
Let's do it again.

POETRY AND LIFE

Poetry is a thought
That has been touched with music.
Words have sounds.
Colors. Flavors.
Personality.

Poetry is the art of
Exclusion
Not unlike life itself.

Sometimes there are
Symmetrical moments in life.
Like Greek architecture
Classical
Peaceful
The balance brings comfort.

But within the symmetrical temple
One finds the asymmetrical statue
Each benefits the other
Too much symmetry
Too much safety
Becomes a tomb of boredom.

Life does not always have
Equal rhythms
In irregularity
There is a certain beauty.

A poem must flow freely
Or we stumble over it.

POKEY PATERNO

Pokey was much more than a cute, little white poodle.
She was a personality.
Michael inherited Pokey when his Mother died.
Pokey already was old.
Had cataracts and diabetes
Requiring daily shots.
Her future looked dim.
Until Michael and Debbie stepped in
And loved Pokey back to life.

They shared two-and-a-half years together
She was combed and fluffed.
Petted and hugged.
Taken for walks and rides to the horse farm.

A little menace in the paddock
She cavorted happily underfoot.
Happiness was Duchess and Pokey,
A day in the country.

Pokey adapted to August in Vermont.
Learning her limits to the edge of the porch.
Summer naps in the hammock
Evening walks along the dirt road.
Shopping in Woodstock.

A last fall and winter warm by the fire
When soon before spring
Came the call to begin a new life again.

She leaves us with love
For all that was done
To make her last years
Such memorable ones.

THE POWER OF CHOICE

It doesn't have to be that way
You can choose another way
If you mean it
Really want to change
The power to do it
Is there.
Put power behind
A new way
Transforming power
Believe in it
Trust not ambivalence.
Put your trust
In the power to transform
What is yours
By faith.
In yourself.

PREGNANT

She was pregnant
With a poem
She felt it coming
In her home.
An in-home birth
No midwife there
To greet this poem
Borne on the air.

As all poems born
From life therein
Reach for light
In ecstasy.

THE PRICE OF A POEM

Everything has its price
'Tis said
But she knew that to be
Untrue.
Not everything
Not everyone
Can be bought.
Sometimes there is no price
Because all would not be enough
To buy
Such virtue.
Above and
Beyond
Price.
There is such a thing.
There is such a thing.

PROJECT PLAN

I project planned my life.
Followed a guiding star
Left it up to the universe
To tell me who I am.

From creation onward
I have served
In various venues
To do my part
My mantra
This all would I choose.

Past and present
All are one
Mix in the future too
And enjoy what follows
As you learn
The authentic
Essential
You.

REFUGE

What a refuge I found
In friendship.
Affection and support
Authenticity
Someone to talk with
Someone to laugh with
Cry with
Travel with
A person for all seasons.
She shared with me her perspectives on life.
Many different from mine
That expanded mine
Into greater confidence
In the mathematics of the universe.

REMEMBER

I see now
What I couldn't see then
It comes back to me
In real time.
Richer
Fuller
Deeper
Happiness.
Know when you have her
Each moment there
Ever so rare
Only now
Do you bring
It back to me
And I tingle
At the remembrance
So long ago
But near to me
Now.
Recaptured
To play the memory of that time
On the record of my mind.

REMEMBRANCE
(For Robert Fletcher
Washington, D.C.
November 1999)

He had a gift for drawing
In childhood,
Evident to his classmates and teachers.
We were proud of him then
As now.
He was a quiet, gentle boy
Liked by all
Modest and self-effacing,
And grew into a gentle man.

Representational art was not in vogue.
Bob chose a career
In commercial art
While he continued to paint
With the same precision
As his first drawings,
But in a new medium,
Water colors.
He made it look easy,
As all fine professionals do,
And his friends marveled
At the detail and realism of his work.

Then a subject as grand as his gifts
Inspired him
American wars.

Their drama. Battles. Funerals.
In a realism that broke our hearts.
Within four years Bob had a body of work
That captured official notice.

Here we are today
In Washington, D.C.
Where Bob's exquisite paintings
Will be shared with many more.
As we cross into a new millennium
These paintings remind us
To reflect on a pivotal time in our history
More than a century ago,
That has brought America to today.
A legacy of remembrance.

RESURRECTION DAY

Here again
Resurrection Day.
Easter.
Spring.
Renewal.
Rising again from
The winter of the soul.
But more than this
Spiritually
It represents
The actual resurrection
From the dead
Of the Christ Consciousness
Come to tell us
We, too, shall rise
To join Him
Not only then
But now
In newness of life.
Ours for the believing.

THE REUNION

It was the 55th reunion
Of the class of 49
From Hawthorne High.

A loyal bunch
They'd met every decade
Since
Until now
When it was divided.
Five year units
Seemed more seemly
Under the circumstances.

Those circumstances
Being our age now
Seventy-three for most of us.

How long could we
Look good enough
To recognize one another
Not that it mattered.
To attendees
We wore nametags
And exclaimed
In wonder
When we found
Our old selves.

The time between
No longer seems
The half-century ago
Before our lives began.

Now nearer the end
We met again
To say how much it meant
To know and grow
A lifetime through
And still remember when.

Or will we meet again?

RIVERSIDE PARK

Nature enveloped me
In her arms
As I sat on the park bench
Taking in the garden
Visual gulps
Of fading fall
Flowers
A mellow sun
Kissed our
Upturned faces.
The hawk flew
Ahead of us
Into the trees
We drank in the air
Nature's perfume
A walk in the park
A fall afternoon.

ROBYN

The spot had long been empty
That place right near my heart
Reserved for dogs from long-gone times
When peace around me flowed.
Nor knew I of the future
Your warm brown eyes did tell
To bring me back
To carefree days
When known
That all is well.

ROCKEFELLER CENTER CHRISTMAS TREE

Welcome to New York, dear tree
But I can tell you're sad
Your trunk is sore from being cut
And you are feeling bad.

For three-quarters of a century
You had another home
Friends of field and feather
Now you are alone.

But look, my dear
There are trees here
Some birds and flowers, too
Reaching out to comfort
And be friends with you.

They'll watch you rise
Be put in place
To be the favorite tree
For thousands of New Yorkers
And even on TV
Seen far across the sea.

You might have been by
Lightning struck
And burned for firewood
The end does come for each of us
But know you're understood.

You'll tell your tale when this is done
And back to woods you go
To serve as mulch among your kind
And dream of Christmas glow.

ROSE

I chose you long ago
In a far off land
To come with me below
To leave the spirit world
Awhile
For bodies we could know
And so we did
For four score and more
To live and learn and love
Together then
Together now
Until we're called above
Together again.

RUINS
(Pelham Bay)

We walked into the dawn
On a day before the
Old year ends
Dawn at Pelham Bay.
The air was brisk
The ground was hard
The squirrels, frisky.
Past the tennis court
Past the stadium
With giant statue
Forever watching
Above.
Along the gravel road
To the crumbled sidewalk
Along the bay
The tide in
The sunken boat covered
The jutting rock where seagulls rest
Covered by the sea
Now filled with slumbering ducks
Awakened
Fluttering their wings
Dancing on the water.
Rising
To the sky
Then gliding back
On the water.
A spectacular display

Against the sunrise.
We walk along the sea wall
Past giant rushes
The sun makes a
Path across the water
Seen through the tall rushes
A morning greeting.
Against a clear blue sky.
Ruins, the natives say
We walked amongst the ruins
Grateful for the privacy
Of their quiet majesty.

THE SACRED HEART

I feel, therefore I know
It is the heart that knows
I often struggled with my mind
Never with my heart
Until I understood
The Sacred Heart
Of peace.

SATURDAY MORNINGS

A loaf of
Italian bread
A bottle of red wine
Remind me of
Weekend mornings
With you.
A walk up Bleecker Street
A stop in the bakery
En route to our
Tiny Village apartment,
Sitting on our bar stools
Round the kitchen table
Memories prized
Beyond human price
To go there again
Would really be nice.

THE SEA OF THE MIND

The sound of the surf
Called softly.
Immerse yourself in me
It said.
Follow me into the depths.
I am an element of transformation
Into new life.

To cross the sea of the mind
Is life's greatest adventure.
Perilous but priceless.
An inward journey
With and against the tides
To a distant shore
Where peace
Like the soft sound of the surf
Will welcome you home.

SEA SHELLS

We spent a day on sea shells
A legacy from Aunt Betty.
Thousands of them
Multi-shaped
Multi-colored
From small shells
To starfish
Conch to crab
A world-class collection
Aunt Betty had
Priced out of existence
No buyers we had
So I guess we'll just keep them
To have and to hold.

THE SHADOW

Even Mother Theresa
Had a shadow.
She said
There's a little bit of
Hitler in me.
Hidden to most.
Unacknowledged,
My shadow.
Bringing it to the surface
Is dangerous
Change hurts.
I'm not as good
As I thought.
Easy to run away
From shadow work
Accept shadow.
It will not be quiet
Until I make friends
With this part
Of me.

SHADOWS

Shadows on the green mountain
A late September afternoon
A brisk wind
Envelops me
On my granite seat
High above the house.
I am in Vermont
A special place to our family
For 50 years.
It's crept its way
Into our souls.
I see my sister below
Pulling a few weeds
From her rocky garden.
Our land is hilly too.
Stones are our crop here
But we needed not
The land for table foods
But to renew our spirit.

A SILENT EXPERIENCE

She came for the silence.
Her strength to renew
She let it surround her
In silent review.

Stop Look and Listen
Be quiet, my dear
You cannot receive
Midst the noise in your ear.

The silence lives
The silence speaks
Wordlessly.
Enter the silence
Feel it descend
Cover you invisibly
Like the stones
At Stonehenge.

Sit in the silence
A seat there for you
The sun has arisen
On a new life for you.

THE SIMPLE LIFE

Some would say I had it all
And threw it all away
But all to them and all to me
Were just like night and day.
Like many who had reached the goals
Of work and home success
I knew there must be something more
To earthly life than this.

I stepped into the future to find what that might be
To test the limits of myself far across the sea
In a tiny rural hamlet where I rediscovered me,
Or a part of me unused 'til then I wanted to explore.
The journey was a long one
But its ending's not obscure.

The road to everlasting joy lies in full exhilaration
Of the preciousness of time and then how to savor it.
When life becomes stale like an old loaf of bread
And one covets it not, is filled with despair
One needs to renew and relearn how to live it
Some do so through illness or near-fatal strife
Some through a baby, a new job or new spouse.
But all change themselves or are changed by events
Who find joy again.

SOME THINGS WE'LL NEVER KNOW

It was not a thought
She liked.
She liked things to be tidy
To have an ending
She understood
If not liked.
But with the years
Came circumstances
Outside her control
Curiosity unquenched.
Time would not tell.
I wondered
What happened
To him
To her
About it?
Time would not tell
She had to let go.
Sometimes it's good
To not know
To let go
And let God.

SOMEBODY TO BUY CANDY FOR

She ate very little of it
But it was part of her
Environment to have it near
Where she could easily get to it
Should her candy spirit call
Irritably.
Candy. Cookies. Cake.
Sweet foods of life
Here on Earth. Gratitude
Needed on a day like this.
Labor Day, 2005
A somber one
A nation bowed in sorrow
And shame
Over Katrina, the killer hurricane
That hit all of us
But especially our beloved
Neglected, New Orleans
Gulfport
Biloxi
All the others.
Regrets must be transformed
Into new realities.
New national purpose and will.

SOMERSET

I did not live in his time.
He died in 1965.
I was 34.
Of no interest to him.
He would have liked me, though.
Open minded.
Open hearted.
Not an intellectual
But perceptive
Intuitive.
Knew things
Others didn't
Despite academia
Or because of it.
Their spirits crossed time
And met
In mutual understanding.
Perhaps they could travel together
In this new time.
They both liked to travel.
Why not?
They both liked comfort
Why not?
He could afford it.
So could she.
They set out.
To new frontiers
In the universe.

SOUL SIGHT

We believed in one another
Instantly
No thought needed
Fate. Destiny.
Choice made
Irrevocable.
Love at Soul Sight.

THE SPIRAL OF TIME

She thought about him
In the spiral of time
She couldn't say she
Understood it all
All she knew
Was that she loved him then.
It was not a happy love
Too many problems.
Too many disappointments.
But when they were together
It was great.
Finally the only answer was martyrdom
There were children.
Who came first.
They both were parents.
And died for them
Until another evolution
In the spiral of time.

SPIRITUAL LEGACY

She had no money.
She was the poor relative.
My aunt.
Her face and form
Appears as I remember her.
On the side porch
With my Mother.
With whom she came to live
When she had to.
It couldn't have been easy for her.
She did what she could
All we can do
It was enough.
Her legacy so much more;
"This is the Day the Lord has made.
Let us rejoice and be glad in it."

SPRING

Mindful of the moment
This I asked to be
Enrich my awareness
Fully
May I attentive be
To the voice of nature
Now surrounding me.

Not just look
But listen
Turn the volume on
Watch as spring
Bursts forth again
The rhythm old
As time.

Come to cheer a weary world
Bruised by war and crime
To lift our souls
The flowers bloom
And so do trees
And lilacs fair
Whose fragrance
Fills the air.
Robins are back
A long winter done
As spring sports her magic
And all is reborn.

STILL THE STARS SHINE
(The Zodiac)
Astral Poetry

CAPRICORN

The goat paused
And surveyed her kingdom
From the mountain top.
She saw the wild flowers
Between the cleft
Of the rocks,
The winding river far below.
The grass beneath her
Bleeding feet
Was green and cool
The clouds above pillowy and close.
Her knees buckled
The grass enfolded her
Offering its rest.
She was home.

AQUARIUS

Son of Saturn.
You would not take the love
I was not sure enough of yours
'Til time developed the negative
And darkness filled the hours.

And Saturn's boy
And Saturn's girl
Were enlightened by Uranus.
And understood a depth of love
Only Saturnians know
And earned eternal friendship
From Father Time below.

PISCES

Oh, last of your Age
Of rainbow hue
All of my life lived with you
Imprisoned by self
Sorrow and pain
To learn to find one's self again.
Thank you for the journey
For accompanying me
Let's go now where you promised
Aquarian eternity.

ARIES

Moon of total distraction
How maddeningly attractive you are
Lights in all directions
Most beautiful of stars.
A gleaming diamond in the night
Shines for him who has the sight

To see in her unquenchable soul
All that giveth life.

TAURUS

Thanks for the lilacs
The daffodil - and rose.
Lilies-of-the-valley
Iris near the road
Wisteria on old wood arbor
Hollyhocks by the door
Peonies, poppies, bleeding hearts
These – and many more –
For Grandpa, the gardener
Etched in memory
From my Taurus garden
Mother Earth to me.

GEMINI

He came bearing light.
He did not know it.
He was the message.
He brought himself
And held it out.
She took and breathed
An air so pure
It gave her life
For centuries more.

CANCER

Moon of Mother
Enclosed within thy daughters here
New birth we ask
That we may give
Life to those with whom we live
Until we integrate ourselves
As you would have us be
To take us to the Father
Beside the Crystal Sea.

LEO

She is a chocolate bunny
Soft and velvety
With eyes that melt
With warming rays
Whatever she can see.
The more she looks
The brighter
Becomes the inner light
'Til in and out are equal
And there is no more night.

VIRGO

Virgo – funny Virgo
How dear to me you are.
So fussy. Petty. Practical.
Super hyper-critical
You make it all so hard.
"Hard it is
Until you find the essence of my heart."
Humble hearts are the first to win
Those runners are the start.

LIBRA

My love affair with Libra
I've often tried to break
It asks from me an answer
That I have tried to shake.
Drawn back again by need for air
From that Libran sky
To know again that precious balance
For which my heart has cried
Until I knew I'd found it
And understood just why
I had to look at Libra long
Were I to know that sky.

SCORPIO

And the eagle swooped down
And alighted
Upon the mountain
And spoke.
"May I rest?
I dare not go lower
My home is in the sky
But if I can but stay a time
Your earth will not be dry.
I'll lead you to the water
By teaching you to fly."
And so they flew together
Up beyond the sky
To the supreme fountainhead
His inexhaustible supply.

SAGITTARIUS

Moon of mind
Exalted moon
How glad I am you're mine.
My soul's aglow with laser light
Penetrating darkest night
Breaking on the brightest dawn
Ever dreamed by mortal man
And brought to him by woman.

STILLNESS

Stillness enveloped her
Not a sound
But for quiet raindrops
Falling on leaves
Brilliant Vermont color
Early this year.
She loved silence
As few others seemed to
Not feeling the substance
That quiet can do
Here on the mountain
Far from the road
A squirrel
A bluebird
Wild turkeys
And deer
Delicious aloneness
A wonderful feel.

A time to go inward
Space to explore
An on-the-ground astronaut
Knowing there's more
Where shall I visit
She mused as she flew
Past far distant planets
Inside her view
I should go to Saturn
To see Father Time

It's been ages and ages
I need to review
The lifetimes I've lived
Since I have been home.
The moons welcomed me
And I knelt at his throne.
He bade me come close
And gave me a crown
Blossoms of lilacs
A flower of mine
To remind me of the planet
I'd just left behind.
To travel abroad
In a universe wide
Knowing I always had
Time on my side.

STONEHENGE

She hid in the stone
Invisible shield
Against enemies without
Secure within
Ready for battle.

She had reinforcements now
An army of love
Surrounded her
She yielded to the force
And knew peace.

SULLY

On a cold February afternoon
Captain Sullenberger's aircraft had a confrontation
With a flock of birds.
And lost.

There was nothing for it
But the River Hudson below.
"My aircraft," said Sully
To the first officer
And took control.

La Guardia and Teterboro
Were ruled out. Too far.
The tarmac would be the Hudson.

All he was and what he'd learned
Coalesced
Into his role
To bring his airship in safely
On water
For 152 people.

And he did.
In a marvel of leadership.
A true hero
For a country hungry for one
Looking for miracles.

And knowing when they saw not just a miracle
But the man who produced it.

Thank you, Sully.

TAKE IT TO MY SOUL

She felt very annoyed
At this issue
Rearing its head again
How many times
How many times
She thought
Must I confront this?

Resentment flared
And she let it
Exploring each facet.
Why must I always be bigger
The one to turn the other cheek?
Silence, she knew
Would not fix it.
Nor the cold shoulder.
Convenience was the
Other's strong suit.
While confrontation
Was my weak one.
There was, she knew,
Only one way.
Take it to my soul.

Let love do it for me, she asked.
Fill me with light
So that when I speak
And speak I must
Against this small aggression

The words will be gentle
The words will be kind
And a way found
Each of us can travel
With dignity.

TAKE ME TO IRELAND

Take me to Ireland
She breathed
Oh, take me home.
What am I doing
That's more important
To me
Than to be there
I'm homesick
For that land
Across the Irish Sea.

Can we not recreate it
In heaven
Just as I knew it then
To live it again
The wish near her heart
Told her it was
Okay with them.

TELEPATHY

Are people in spirit
Available all the time?
Can I reach you now?
Please let me know when
We can chat
Because I know not how.

How can I be ready
When you would call on me?
Teach me how together
Telepathically we can be.

I will call your name
At a time you'll hear.
Hello
Your answer
Will connect us on that plane.

TELL ME WHY YOU LIKE IT HERE

Because it is the geography
Nearest to my biology
My body's aching longing
Here finds rest
On a lightly warm
October field
A sunset afternoon
The mountain purple-shadowed now
Against the cloudless blue
The hills ablaze with foliage
Of every golden hue
The grass that special shade of green
Known to a favored few
Who recognized the pearly gates
The moment they stepped through.

THANKSGIVING DAY 1983

A gray November morning
A light drizzle
Fell on Macy's Parade.
Helium giants
On side streets
Waiting their turns
To march.
A fat clown
In outrageous costume
Sat on a bench
In front of the Planetarium.
Christmas floats
And songs
Filled the air.
Balloons
Of Mickey Mouse
And reindeer
Added color and
Beckoned the
Children
In all of us.
The crowds
Were enormous.
No way to cross
At the Dakota.
Claustrophobia
Threatened
But the crowd
Was calm.

I retraced my
Entrance and
Broke free
At 81st Street
I slipped
Into the park
To the Boathouse
Where a jelly donut
And black coffee
Reminded me of home.
Alone at Thanksgiving.
But not alone.
A stranger
At a table nearby
Reading the paper.
The two of us
Enjoying the silence
And the view.
The sparrows
Hovered near
Hoping for crumbs.
Now a pram
With nanny.
She dips his
Pacifier into
Her coffee.
He likes it
And soon wants more.
The music sounds
In the distance
As the parade
Moves down
Central Park West.

34

She would have been 34.
I cannot see her there
Left us at 10.
My godchild.
A magical one
We knew one another
For ages back then
Reunited here
For special mention.
Ten but counting
Work finished, done
Leaving her spirit
To inspire us some
From one who saw hunger
And misery
Even though young.
Even though young.
And vowed to help heal it
From dimensions above
On this, that earthly birthday,
Best wishes and love.

TIME

It's only a matter of time, he said ominously.
He said many things ominously.
So many ominous times became not serious to me.
He loved the end of the world
The Apocalypse.
It was a characteristic of our relationship.
Drama.
I got accustomed to it
And determined to change my role
In this play of life.

It's never too late, I said.
I come from a planet where time is abundant.
Take my word for it.
There's enough time.
I am a daughter of the Master of Time,
Father Saturn.
I understand time.
It is true this time one day shall be no more
In one reality.
Like all times everywhere in the universe
They begin and end.
And beyond them there is a new time.
Time itself is ageless.
But there are indeed many times
One follows another.
Taken together, we call them eternity.

TIME IS THE PEN

That marks our days
More aware now
Of endings
New beginnings
Our steps a bit slower now.
Let us remember
The times that are past
Close always
As we go on
To new life.
Without you.
With you
Always.

TIMELESS TRUTHS

Beset on every side
Adversity
Betrayal
Disappointment
Sorrow
Dark companions indeed
Surrounded her.
These must be here by invitation
She reflected.
No doubt my own.
Why have I summoned them
She wondered?
What must I change within myself
To have them go quickly?
She thought of the old hymn
"Lord, lead me on to higher ground.
A higher ground than I have found."
She knew it was out there.
She wanted to go there.
What she did have
Was the light of her own faith
To lead the way.
It was all she needed, she knew.
It had never failed.
It would light the darkness
And disperse it
Into a new dawn.
With a brand-new view.

TO ONE ANOTHER ON OUR GOLDEN WEDDING ANNIVERSARY
(For Aunt Ruth and Uncle Fran)

Fifty years
Of togetherness
Our Golden Wedding Day
Fifty times
November's come
Since you came to stay.
Fifty winters
Fifty springs
Fifty summers
Shared with you
To greet this day
This milestone
On our eternal way
To remember the years
One by one
Since that fall day
When we were wed.
A kaleidoscope of memories
Tumbles down the years
Good times
Lean times
Laughter
Tears.
A half-century of memories

Of one another
Five decades with you.
Thank you, dear.
Thank you, dear.

TOGETHER AGAIN

The lilacs are gone, Mother
Mowed down.
They hardly bloomed, she said
And she couldn't see.
They were in the way.

They lie dead in a field
As you do.
You died together.
And are, I know, together again.
Lilacs blooming all the time
Surrounding you with their lavender
And spring fragrance
Filled with birds of song.

The Vermont I knew with you.
And the lilacs.
Went together.
They could not stay.
The heart of the house was gone.
They went with you.
A gigantic bouquet.
Together again.

TRADITIONS OF CHRISTMAS

She was captured
By the traditions of Christmas
A love – hate relationship.
Driven to do it all
The decorations
The cards
The special food treats
The homemade cheese balls
Peanut butter dates
The presents wrapped
Perfectly
With the right ribbon
Bows and seal.
No shortcuts for her.
Always one more thing
She would have it no other way
Christmas again.
A candlelight service
Hark the Herald Angels Sing.

TROUBLE

The universe sent me Trouble
With a capital T.
Trouble came my way.
Make the best of it
My dear
It's not your lucky day
You'll learn how to live with it
Objective you must be
No doubt a cosmic reason
Happened so for me.

TRUTH

She spoke her truth
It hit its mark
An arrow straight and sure
I knew at once the right of it
Because her heart is pure.

I hated to be wrong
But wrong indeed I was.
Repentance first
Forgiveness
Is the way of love.

The night it seemed
Had an interesting theme
The clash of cultures old
To love and learn from each of them
A story yet untold.

TWIN

Because I'd always had her
I was not really conscious
Of life without her
Or perhaps the merest thought of it
Was too unbearable
And I did not let it enter my heart.
When it did at last
And I understood the magnitude of
The gift of a twin
This twin
And knew once again
In time
The love of God
From age to age
As we meet again.

As we have before
And always will
My heart gives thanks
For its greatest blessing
In this time
On this Planet
Rose.

UNDERSTAND ME

I wish I understood me more
She mused.
But was put off
By possible consequences.
Like Pandora's box
What will I find
But true to one's kind?
Surrender more
To gain more
Understanding of me.

UNITED NATIONS GARDEN

Sweet Surrender. Friendship. Peace. Magic. Touch of Class. These names of roses wove a spell about me as I walked alone in the Rose Garden of the U.N., the third of December, 1988. They played over and over on the record in my mind – rotating roses in pink, yellow, white. From a bench under a pale sun, I looked down the rows of bare Japanese cherry trees planted deep in ivy – blowing softly silver in the mild breeze. The Brooklyn Bridge downriver outlined against the sky. Grass greener than springtime. A December garden in New York.

UNIVERSITY OF ADVERSITY

Most of us have attended
The University of Adversity.
No one ever graduates
It's a lifelong school.
But some do well
Others fail to find
The answer to adversity
Is found within the climb.

Like the pearl within the clam
Its grain an irritation
Forming it as planned.
The mighty oak
From a seedling grew
Against all nature's ills
To stand tall
Against the wind and rain
A triumph o'er adversity.

So it is with all life
Growth that gives us pain
Is the path that leads us
Through adversity.

It will end well
In its time
A time we may not see
Believing good will come from it
Is the key to adversity.

VERMONT

It was a summer
Rich in clover
And Queen Anne's Lace.
From behind the lilacs
And the stone wall
Beside the wild roses
My eyes took in it all
Feasting on the meadows
The old apple trees
The dirt and grassy driveway
All are dear to me.
The mountain peak
In distance
Blue against the sky
Filled with puffy pillows
Playfully passing by
The hum of bees on clover
An airplane on high
Country sounds of August
Butterflies nearby.
Maples turning rosy
Blackberries finishing up
The sun shone hot
And warmed my soul.
As nature filled my cup.

THE VERMONTER

No. 56
The Amtrak train to Randolph
To be met by my sister.
Vermont.

Second home for
Fifty years
Early spring
Summer
Early fall
But not winter.
I took the
Long train ride
Eight hours.
Sometimes longer.
Derailments
Floods
Accidents
Trees on the track.

She had her rituals
Penn Station
The Passenger Waiting Room
Coffee and a jelly donut.
People watching.
Despite all
Police instruction
We watched each other's luggage
So we could get the paper.

Or go to the loo.
Took turns coaxing the dispatcher
So we could board early
For a seat not too far from the café car.
And where we could see our luggage.
The old black waiter remembered me.
I bought cheese, Doritos and asked for a glass of ice.
I always brought my two little bottles of vodka
At the liquor store in New York
For half the train price.
It was a comfort to know I had a
Good picnic along.
Tuna sandwiches
Oatmeal raisin cookies
Apples and nectarines
Or Swiss candy bar
Water.
I once heard about a train twelve hours delayed
With no food.
I only ate one sandwich and the coffee.
I bought a cup of tea and for dinner a cup of soup.
Despite the heat outside this July day
It was frigid on the train.
I always wore a suit against the air conditioning.
NY - CT - MA -VT - NH - VT again.
I read my book.
Sometimes looked at the scenery
Or talked to a passenger.
Until White River.
Almost there.
She wanted to see the villages she knew so well.
Royalton.
Bethel.
Randolph. My stop.

VETERANS DAY

What is a vet, anyway?
One who has survived a war.
We're all veterans, she thought,
Of our former selves
Former battles
Other times.
History now.
But remembered.

Some vets like war.
Never happier
Volunteer again.
Warriors.
Vets of many wars.

Weary now
Ready for peace
Ready for peace
In me.

THE VIBRATION OF THE DAY

She knew there was a
Vibration for the day
The aspects told her
How they held sway.
Enter you into them
Go where they go
Join the vibration
By just letting go
They'll take you in
Like a carousel ride
Ride with the music
Follow the tide
Of a day made for everyone
Who can follow the vibe.

VIVID EXPERIENCE

What was your most
Vivid experience
He asked?
I'd had so many
I had to think for a moment.
I knew.
It was you, Frank.
Hands down
It was you,
Dear.
It was you.

WAR BACKPACK

I had such a good time
Getting together my
Backpack for war
I'm ashamed to admit.
I followed much of
Mr. Homeland Security's list
Of emergency supplies
But it was woefully short
Of things a person needs.
Like passport and money
Washcloth and wipes
Change of clothes
Ibuprofen, of course
Imodium and band-aids
Moisturizer, shampoo, too.
Block for the sun.
All these and more are needed
For life on the run.

Too heavy this pack if needed
To carry far
But at last assembled
And easy to find.
Laughing, I wasn't
Serious indeed
But still I enjoyed
Packing for war.
Power bars. Hershey bars, cheese crackers
Corned beef and tuna

Like getting ready for a picnic.
Under a dark cloud.
Flashlights and batteries
Swiss Army knife
All this I must carry
When I flee for my life.

WATCHING THE CLOCK

Over sixty now
And watching the clock
Tick toward the Big R.
Retirement.
Not from life of course
But The Office.
The Office.
More home than home
For more than 40 years.
It was not just a job.
It was an identity
Most else
Came second.
Why was that, she wondered?
She knew she was not alone
In having invested so much
Of herself
In the structure of the office.
It was a living thing, really.
It seemed to understand her.
It provided shelter from the storms of life.
Sometimes the storms
Erupted within the office
And chaos and confusion reigned.
She would take a respite then
'Til peace returned.
Her office was a vehicle
Of endless opportunities
For self-expression

Of her best self.
Her closest friends were made there.
Her life crossed hundreds.
Changing her.
Changing them.
Such a good friend, The Office.
A microcosm of the Big Office
Out there
Of which she would always be a part.
So, she could leave soon
Assured of her legacy.

WATERS OF SORROW

It was a long time after
But grief still fresh at times
As it always would be.
Love doesn't die.

She let the waters of sorrow
Flow over her
Sweet sorrow
In memories
Of good times shared
Only with you.
Back for a visit
To a love that was true.

WE NEED MORE IRISH DAYS

Across the hills
Down through the dales
Floating over time
They came.

Gaelic melodies.

Pure as the air from
Whence they came.
Dancing on the winds of sound
To reach their own.

Sons of morning.
Daughters of dawn.

WHAT IF NOW IS HEAVEN?

What if now is heaven?
Have we failed to see
That what is now before us
Is a piece of eternity.
Hell it can be just as well
If we cannot see
That whatever happens
Even acts of God
Ours to meet
With equanimity.

WHAT IS

To give birth to the new

We must let go of what was
To open the door to new beginnings.
To hold on to the energy of what is
Keeps it from changing.
Some things we can change.
Some things we cannot.
Surrender to what we cannot
Believe the evolutionary process
Is at work
Leading us and the world forward
As we trust in evolutionary intelligence.

WHAT'S IT LIKE AT 75?

Different than I expected.
There seems to be a kind of wisdom that descends
A distillation of the years before.
A new me.
Enhanced by experience and explorations.

She noticed things not seen before
For which she'd had no time.
Time was now available.

Solitude was mine.
Small is big
And big is small
So it is all the same
Enter into the moment
And call it by its name.

WHITE RABBIT

She comes to you in purity
With words to cheer you on.

She represents fertility
In all its myriad forms.

She knows her way
Through briar patch
And where to go in storms.

Productive is her winning suit
She'll share her secrets, too.
If each morning you will call
She'll have a chat with you.

WILD FLOWERS

Have you never kissed a wild flower
Nor held one tenderly
Looked into its own dear face
And have one look at you?
To fall in love with flowers
Is to have lovers everywhere
Were I to have a wish today
'Twould be the Flower Queen.

WORKMATES

A chemistry
Between them
Like table tennis
She returned his serve
They weren't in love
Really
Except what is love
But a many-splendored thing
He always said.
Different.
Creative.
A love that brought peace.
A many-splendored thing.

WORK PARTNERS

They were
Long-time
Work partners.
There was a
Synchronicity
Between them.
He knew what
He wanted.
She knew how to get it.
Great ideas
Great implementation.
Not only that.
They could reverse
Their roles.
Soul mates.

THE WRITING PROCESS

You want I should tell you about the process?

Do I know it myself?

I draw upon the sum total
Of my experiences and observations.
I believe in them.
I surrender to them.
And receive inspiration from them.

When the inspiration strikes
I pay attention.
Make it my No. 1 priority
And write it down
On whatever I can find.

Often my checkbook
Business cards
Grocery ads
And sometimes a small pad
I carry for the purpose
If I remember it.

But if the inspiration is not captured
Not to worry.
There'll be other times.

ZENE DEKALIM
(Gaza)

Sadness came.
Overwhelming sorrow
Asked to give back
My land.
My home. My children's home.
Here in Gaza.
Taken in war
Given back for peace.

Like soldiers
We were asked to die
For peace.
We surrendered
To force.

THE ZOO GIRL

She came to see her friends.
Her heart was always sad.
Sometimes the heat was too heavy
Her friends had nowhere to flee
They flicked off the flies and inwardly cried
For the time when they had been free.

Or worse it was chill
And the space smaller still
No place to go but above
And they looked from the bars
To the heart of a friend
With eyes of infinite love.

And sometimes she saw it
And told them she knew
And wanted to touch them and play
Their answer was yes
But no one believed
Or would open the cage
On the grass and the trees and the sky.
The brooks and the rocks
Would all have to wait
Until love makes the fear in us die.

ABOUT THE AUTHOR

From banking to philanthropy to publishing, Evelyn C. Walsh has enjoyed a wide-ranging professional career, most recently as co-author with Dr. Verne S. Atwater of the book *A Memoir of the Ford Foundation: The Early Years 1936-1968*. Her first book of poetry, *The Time Clock Zodiac*, was published in 2004.

Walsh was added to the *Who's Who of American Women* in 1981 and was among an early group of senior executives elected to the YWCA's Academy of Women Achievers. Now retired and the mother of a grown daughter, Walsh lives in New York City, where she enjoys reading, travel, metaphysics, astrology, children and architecture.

www.ingramcontent.com/pod-product-compliance
Lightning Source LLC
Chambersburg PA
CBHW022058090426
42743CB00008B/647